What Can You Do with a Major in

BIOLOGY?

What Can You Do with a Major in

BIOLOGY?

Real people.

Real jobs.

Real rewards.

Bart Astor

Jennifer A. Horowitz,
Series Creator

WILEY

Wiley Publishing, Inc.

For general information on our other products and services or to obtain technical support please contact our Customer Care Department within the U.S. at (800) 762-2974, outside the U.S. at (317) 572-3993 or fax (317) 572-4002.

Wiley also publishes its books in a variety of electronic formats. Some content that appears in print may not be available in electronic books. For more information about Wiley products, please visit our web site at www.wiley.com.

ISBN: 0-7645-7606-2

Library of Congress Cataloging-in-Publication data is available from the publisher upon request.

Printed in the United States of America
10   9   8   7   6   5   4   3   2   1
Book design by LeAndra Hosier
Cover design by Sandy St. Jacques
Book production by Wiley Publishing, Inc. Composition Services

WILEY

Table of Contents

Introduction 1

About This Book 3

Why I Wrote This Book 3

A Guide to This Book 4

1 Majoring in Biology 7

Degrees and Curricula 8

Minor in Biological Sciences 11

Minors in Other Departments and Double Majors 12

College Rankings 13

Colleges Offering Biology Programs 13

Biology 14

Biochemistry 15

Zoology 16

Entrance Requirements 16

Skills and Abilities Required to Succeed in This Major 17

Wrap Up 18

2 Choosing a College for Biology Majors 21

To Parents: 21

To Students: 22

What Admission Officers Look For 23

The Transcript 23

Test Scores 24

The Essay or Personal Statement 25

Extracurricular Activities 25

Recommendations 26

A Final Point About Admission 27

Paying for the College of Your Choice 27

Access and Choice 27

Determining Need 29

Cost of Attendance 29

Types of Financial Aid 30

Net Cost versus Sticker Price 31

Is It Worth It? 31

Private Scholarships and Scholarship Search Firms 33

Wrap Up 34

3 **Internships and Attending Graduate School** **35**

Biology Internships 36
    Why Would I Want to Be an Intern? 37
    Will I Get Paid? 38
    How Do I Find an Internship? 38
Graduate School Programs in Biology 39
Graduate School Disciplines 40
Quality Programs and Rankings 42
    Selective Biology Graduate Schools 43
    Highly Ranked Graduate Schools 44
Admission to Grad School 45
Paying for Graduate School 46
    Similarities between Grad and Undergrad 46
    Differences between Grad and Undergrad 47
Is It Worth It? 48
Choices, Choices, Choices 49
Wrap Up 51

4 **Career Possibilities** **53**

Job Descriptions 53
    Health Scientist Administrator 54
    Forester 54
    Medical Instrument Technician 54
    Medical Technologist 54
    Patent Examiner 55
    Sanitarian 55
    Quarantine Officer 55
    Food Scientist 56
    Park Guide 56
    Pharmacologist/Toxologist 56
    Forensic Scientist 56
    Medical Writer 57
    Public Relations, Pharmaceuticals 57
    Agronomist 57
    Archivist, Curator, and Museum Technician 58
    Dietitian and Nutritionist 58
    Sales Representatives 58
    Biologist 59
    Environmental Scientist 61
    Food Scientist 61
    Animal Scientist 62

Medical Librarian 62
Optometrist 63
Podiatrist 63
Chiropractor 64
Audiologist 64
Biomedical Engineer 65
Pharmacist 65
Wrap Up 66

5 Breaking into the Job Market ....**.67**
Planning Ahead 68
Searching for a Job 69
The Basics 69
How to Budget Your Time 69
Your Job Search Book 70
Don't Believe the Clichés 71
Stay Informed and Be Realistic 72
Take Advantage of Current Trends 73
How to Network 75
Online Job Searches 77
Preparing Your Résumé 78
Career Center, On-Campus Recruiters, and Career Fairs 80
Find Your Own Job Openings 81
Interviewing for a Job 82
Do Your Research 82
Practice 83
Interview Tips 84
The Interview and Follow Up 84
Wrap Up 86

6 Case Studies ....**.87**
Karen, Epidemiologist 87
What I Do 88
Why I Majored in Biology 88
How the Biology Major Prepared Me for My Job 89
Other Training 89
Helpful Moves 90
Pitfalls to Avoid 91
What I Love About My Job 91
Things on the Job I Could Do Without 91
My Work and My Life 92

Salaries for Epidemiologists 92
Some Thoughts About Karen's Career 92
Susan: Education and Outreach Program Manager 93
What I Do 93
Why I Majored in Biology 94
How the Biology Major Prepared Me for My Job 94
Other Training 94
Helpful Moves 95
Pitfalls to Avoid 95
What I Love About My Job 95
Things on the Job I Could Do Without 96
My Work and My Life 96
Salaries for Epidemiologists 96
Some Thoughts About Susan's Career 96
Sara, Zookeeper/Biologist in the Birdhouse 97
What I Do 97
Why I Majored in Biology 98
How the Biology Major Prepared Me for My Job 98
Other Training 99
Helpful Moves 99
Pitfalls to Avoid 100
What I Love About My Job 100
Things on the Job I Could Do Without 100
My Work and My Life 101
Salaries for Zookeepers 101
Some Thoughts About Sara's Career 101
Rick, Science Reporter 102
What I Do 102
Why I Majored in Biology 103
How the Biology Major Prepared Me for My Job 103
Other Training 103
Helpful Moves 104
Pitfalls to Avoid 105
What I Love About My Job 105
Things on the Job I Could Do Without 105
Salaries for Reporters 106
Some Thoughts About Rick's Career 106
My Work and My Life 106
Katie, Healthcare Attorney 107
What I Do 107
Why I Majored in Biology 108

How the Biology Major Prepared Me for My Job 108
Other Training 109
Helpful Moves 109
Pitfalls to Avoid 109
What I Love About My Job 110
Things on the Job I Could Do Without 110
My Work and My Life 110
Salaries for Attorneys 111
Some Thoughts About Katie's Career .111
Gail, Technical Director, Hospital Laboratory 111
What I Do 112
Why I Majored in Biology 112
How the Biology Major Prepared Me for My Job 112
Other Training 113
Helpful Moves 113
Pitfalls to Avoid 113
What I Love About My Job 114
Things on the Job I Could Do Without 114
My Work and My Life 114
Salaries for Epidemiologists 115
Some Thoughts About Gail's Career 115

7 **Final Thoughts** **117**

Appendix: Resources **119**
Biology Honor Society 119
Professional Resources 119
The American Institute of Biological Sciences (AIBS) 120
Professional Societies 120
Job Listing Web Sites 121
College Admission, Search, and Financial Aid Resources 122
Biology Career Reference Books 123

Index **125**

Foreword

What can I do with a major in biology?

Can you give me a list of jobs I can do if I major in biology?

Should I major in X and minor in Y or major in Y and minor in X to be sure I'll get a great job?

How often I've heard these questions as a career counselor at a traditional liberal arts college. Concerns about "the major" are consuming to students from their first year through their last. At first it is the anxiety over choosing the "perfect" major; later it is concern that the major chosen may not have been the right decision.

Gone are the days when students felt they could major in anything they chose with no concern about their future careers. Managerial training programs that welcomed bright college graduates regardless of their academic backgrounds are rarely seen, and the world seems to get more and more specialized and require greater and greater focus and preparation from college graduates.

This series of books should ease much of the anxiety around the choice of major through its thoughtful exploration of possible career paths that lead directly from a specific major or which may on first glance seem completely unrelated. Much can be learned from the personal histories of individuals who majored in particular fields as well as from the rich resources in the Appendix.

Career development is a messy process. It can be seen as a dialogue between the self and the world. It involves interests, skills, values, and dreams. It requires an individual to be able to articulate her or his assets whether they are transferable skills, abilities honed through jobs and internships, passions fueled by community service—and whatever one has chosen for a solid academic foundation—one's major.

— *Jane Celwyn*
Director of the Office of Career Development
Barnard College, New York

Introduction

What kinds of jobs can I get if I major in biology? (Other than being a doctor, of course.) What if I really love biology but also love other subjects? Can I major in one and minor in another? And just what is a biology major? What courses do I have to take? What can I do after I graduate?

How often counselors and admission officers have heard these questions. Concerns about choosing the right major consume students from their first years in high school through their last years in college—and sometimes beyond. At first it is the anxiety over choosing the "perfect" college; later it is concern that the college chosen may not have been the right decision. Throughout, there is the concern and pressure not only to choose the right college, but also the perfect major!

Guess what? There is *no* perfect college. And there's also *no* perfect major. If you learn anything from this book, it's that. You can get an excellent education at many colleges.

Second, just because you choose to major in biology in your freshman or sophomore year doesn't mean you're locked in. If you choose your college based on its biology program, for example, and later decide that you would prefer some other major—or some other college—that, too, will be okay. Or if you start out with a liberal arts major or at a liberal arts college and realize that you really love biology, it's never too late to change your direction—or your school.

Some may disagree with that philosophy. They argue that students should make their educational decisions based on their future careers because the world has become so specialized and competitive that a broad education isn't enough.

In my opinion, that's just not so! Sure the world is more complicated and competitive. And students need all the legs up they can get to succeed. But a background in one area, especially in a science, qualifies you to go on to a wide choice of careers and specialties. I will show you in this book some examples of people who did just that. They majored in biology but are not necessarily working as biologists.

A good science background provides expertise in fundamentals that can be applied to most careers. Managers in business settings, for example, often use the knowledge they gained in statistics courses that most science majors are required to take. They do so to interpret data and create and analyze budgets. And they will use the skills involved in doing team science projects successfully to work as a member or leader of a team. You'll see later in the case studies presented in Chapter 6 that a good foundation in science, specifically biology, opens up a wide range of possible careers.

That's not to belittle the importance of choosing a college or major that's right for you. You just should keep in mind that your whole life is *not* determined by decisions you make as a 17 or 18 year old.

The career path you choose is rarely fixed. It is influenced by the experiences to which you are exposed and your interests, skills, values, and dreams. Choosing a college and a major requires that you articulate your strengths, transferable skills, abilities honed through jobs and internships, passions fueled by community service, and the thirst to learn more about a subject. That will often lead you to choosing your major. And if it's related to one of the biological sciences, this book can help you.

This series of books should ease much of the anxiety around the choice of major by showing you the possible career paths that lead directly from a specific major or that might on first glance seem completely unrelated. You can learn much from the personal histories of individuals who majored in particular fields as well as from the rich resources in the appendix.

About This Book

This book is part of a series of major-based career guides. In this chapter, you will learn the rationale behind the series, see how the book is organized, and find out how to make it work for you.

WHY I WROTE THIS BOOK

When I was growing up, everyone assumed I would major in the subject in which I did best in high school: mathematics. I clearly had an aptitude for math and had scored high on the SAT. So it made sense to choose my college and major based on those facts. I never even considered any other areas. When everyone I met asked me the same questions:

♦ What colleges are you applying to?

♦ What are you going to major in?

I had a ready answer for them. As it turned out, I should have given these decisions a lot more thought. After my first semester in college, I realized that I never really understood what it meant to be a math major. And when I did, I also realized that what I had chosen was not right for me. So, like many students, I changed my major. As a result, I put a lot of stress on myself (and my family) and had to scramble to meet all the requirements to graduate in the requisite time period. Fortunately for me, I was able to resume my studies at the same college. But it was a lesson learned.

During that frantic time when I was confused, I envied those who always knew what they wanted to be and were able to choose their major—and their school—easily. In high school it probably appeared that I was one of those whom others, who were less sure of their choices, probably envied. If they only knew!

The fact is most kids in high school don't know for sure what they want to do for their life's work, or even what they want for the next four years. Furthermore, most don't even know what it means to major in biology, just as I didn't know about math. An area like biology has many, many different fields. Yet all most of us know about biology in high school is dissecting frogs, some basic genetics, some anatomy and physiology, and a lot more about plants than we ever thought we would care to know. Oh, but there's so much more.

That's partly what this book addresses. We will show you the kinds of curricula that biology majors take. We'll discuss some of the specialties within the field of biology. And we'll talk to some people who majored in biology and now use the knowledge they gained in jobs other than biologist, biology teacher, or doctor. You might be surprised at just how far-reaching and applicable that knowledge can be. You'll also be surprised at the kinds of jobs for which someone who majored in biology qualifies.

Of course, most people think that biology is essentially a premed major. Although in some colleges that may be so, in most it is not. Premed has pretty much become its own specialty now, with different graduation requirements. Clearly there is a great deal of overlap. But in this book, we will not deal with premed but strictly biology.

Many high school students are concerned about the kinds of jobs that will be available after they graduate from college. College costs have risen dramatically, even at the state colleges, and borrowing large sums to pay for school has become a way of life. This is true for students as well as their families. As a result, students are choosing their colleges and their majors by first taking into account their marketability upon graduation and their expected ability to pay back their loans. As a biology major, you will certainly be in an excellent position to secure a good job, one that has a decent pay scale, at least compared to some other areas of specialty (philosophy, English, and so on). But salary is still a significant concern. We will address some of that concern and hope to put your mind at ease.

A Guide to This Book

Following are the features you will find in this book. Obviously not all areas will be appropriate to all readers. Some of you are high school students making that first decision; some are current college students now having to declare a major; some are current college students in the midst of rethinking their choices. And some are parents of students who want to be able to support their children's decisions. Notice I said, *support* their children's decision, not help them make it. I'll talk more about that when we discuss choosing a college.

In Chapter 1, we will talk specifically about what it means to be a biology major. We will look at and compare the curricula at a couple of colleges: a highly rated, selective university and one not so selective. The point of this is to show you the kinds of courses you will take and the fields of study available to you when you major in biology. I'll also give you a little insight into what it will be like when you major in bio, address at least one of the questions asked earlier—that is, is it possible to switch your major? And we'll talk about other options for you, including majoring in two disciplines and minoring in biology while majoring in something else, or the opposite.

In Chapter 2, we will get more specific and look at the decision-making process involved with choosing a college in which you will major in biology. Here we will also mention some things about the costs associated with attending college, including some expenses that are specific to those majoring in bio. And we will provide you with some tips on choosing and applying to colleges and on paying for your education. We will *not* rank colleges. That is not our purpose here. Instead, our intention is to give you some guidance in what to look for when you are evaluating biology programs at various colleges and universities.

In Chapter 3, we'll focus on what's next, that is, what's ahead for you after you graduate with a degree in biology. I'll provide a current prospective for future graduates with an undergraduate or graduate degree in biology. We'll talk about the job prospects in the near future as well as the salaries that you can expect. And we discuss going on to graduate school. I'll address the factors determining graduate admission, how much it will cost and how you can pay, recognizing that graduate school financing is quite different than undergraduate school.

When you decide you're ready to leave college after you finished your studies, then Chapter 4 is where we'll discuss the kinds of career possibilities for bio majors. I'll mention the obvious jobs, certainly, but also show you some related careers that you may not have thought of but where biology majors are working. Then in Chapter 5, I'll show you some job-seeking ideas that have helped other bio majors secure interesting and challenging jobs.

Then we get to the real-life examples of people who majored in bio as undergraduates and are now working in related careers. Here we'll ask them to talk about their lives. They'll explain what they do, why they chose to major in bio, what other training they did, and what they love (and don't love) about their jobs.

Do you know you want to major in bio? Or are you a little mixed up about it? If so, here's where we hope you can really get some insight into what you can imagine as you are now choosing a major.

Finally, in the appendix, I'll provide you with some resources to help you make your decision about whether to major in bio and the kinds of organizations and societies that exist for graduates and professionals.

After reading this book, I hope you will see that there are ways to make a living from a major in biology that you might not have thought of. And although some careers may be the logical or even stereotypical careers associated with a biology major, others are quite innovative, unusual, and perhaps ones you've never even heard of. But they all depended on the knowledge acquired from majoring in bio. Keep an open mind; you never know where it will take you!

Chapter 1

Majoring in Biology

There is probably no area of specialization in today's world undergoing more change than the field of biology. Dramatic progress has revolutionized the science, and approaches using mathematics, chemistry, physics, and technology have led to extraordinary changes in the method of teaching biology. As a result, you will see wide disparity in the curricula at different schools, depending on the degree to which the university is a world leader in research. There will almost always be some kind of core curriculum essential to building a student's breadth of knowledge in bio.

In this book we will focus on that core since the breadth of instruction is so wide. And as new areas of exploration open new frontiers, not every college will offer every specialty within biology. In some ways that will make your choice of college harder and in some ways easier. If, for example, you are an A student with an interest and work experience in, for example, genetic engineering, your choices of curriculum will be limited to those colleges offering opportunities for advanced research in highly specialized fields. In contrast, if you are in high school and, like most of your classmates, did well and enjoyed your high school biology classes, may have even taken Advanced Placement courses, and think you want to major in biology, you may be looking for a curriculum that offers a broader scope of courses. In that case you will be looking at programs that provide you with a greater overview of the various fields from which you can choose.

Major Fields of Study and Subspecialties in Colleges for Biological Sciences

Anatomy	Molecular Biology
Bacteriology	Neurosciences
Biochemistry	Nutrition, Scientific
Biology, General	Pathology, Human and Animal
Biometrics and Biostatistics	Pharmacology, Human and Animal
Biophysics	Physiology, Human and Animal
Botany, General	Plant Pathology
Cell Biology	Plant Pharmacology
Ecology	Plant Physiology
Embryology	Predentistry
Entomology	Premed
Genetics	Prevet
Histology	Radiobiology
Immunology	Toxicology
Marine Biology	Zoology, General
Microbiology	

(Source: Bureau of Labor Statistics, 2004)

In the accompanying table, you can see the fields of college study under biological sciences in the Bureau of Labor Statistics. Take note that premed is listed as just one of the subspecialties. As I said at the outset, many colleges offer a premed major for those who are looking to enter medicine and become doctors. The curriculum for a premed is usually quite similar to that of bio majors.

Degrees and Curricula

Many colleges with a major in biology, except for the most selective and specialty-oriented, offer two kinds of degrees: a Bachelor of Arts (B.A.) and a Bachelor of Science (B.S.). These two degrees have overlapping but different requirements.

See the sidebar for the requirements for a B.A. degree at an excellent university, but not one considered to be in the very top echelon of colleges.

As you can see, students must take 32 credit hours in biology, including introductory courses, cell biology, animal biology, microbiology, ecology, and genetics. In addition, students aiming for a B.A. take a year of chemistry, a statistics course, and two other science courses.

The B.S. major, on the other hand, requires significantly more science: 12 additional hours of biology, an additional year of chemistry or geology, a year of physics, and an additional year of math.

In contrast, another college—a more selective, prestigious one—offers only one kind of biology degree. At this school, you can complete only a B.S. program, and you must select from among three choices:

◆ Biological sciences (a broad-based major)

◆ Molecular and cellular biology

◆ Ecology, evolution, and organismal biology

B.A. in Biology: Major Requirements

In addition to the general requirements for the B.A. degree, students must present the following:

1. 32 hours of biology including:
   Cell Biology
   Animal Biology
   Plant Biology
   Microbiology
   Ecology
   Genetics
2. One year of chemistry
3. Statistics
4. Two additional courses in other sciences

The core curriculum for all three specialties requires that students take three basic bio courses: introduction to biology, introductory lab work, and genetics, plus one year each of general and organic chemistry, including labs. In addition, depending on which specialty is chosen, students must take 30 hours of biology courses (approximately 10 courses), some of which are lab courses, and an upper-level seminar or independent study. These can be in a variety of subjects depending on the field of specialty: cell biology, biochemistry, botany, zoology, evolution, insect ecology, biology of insects, biological clocks, ecology, plant-animal interactions, statistical methods in biology, molecular evolution, and environmental toxins.

B.S. in Biology: Major Requirements

Students must complete the following in addition to the general education requirements:

1. 44 hours of biology including:
   Cell biology
   Animal biology
   Plant biology
   Microbiology
   Ecology
   Genetics
2. One year of general chemistry and one semester of organic chemistry.
3. One of the following:
   a) The second semester of organic chemistry.
   b) One upper-level, three-credit chemistry course.
   c) Geology 101 and 102. Students are encouraged to consult with a biology faculty advisor to ascertain which option best meets their career goals.
4. One year of physics.
5. One year of math and one course in statistics or computer science.

Locating a College Web Site

The best way to ensure that you understand the requirements is to look at the specific schools to which you will be applying. The curricula requirements all appear on the college Web sites or are in their brochures and catalogs. Almost every college will have a Web site, and they are usually found at www.collegename.edu (edu standing for education). Because many colleges have similar initials (such as "OSU," which could be either Oregon, Ohio, or Oklahoma State University), a simple way to find the Web site is to use an Internet search engine. That will help you even when the college has a different Web site name than what you might expect (such as www.wustl.edu for Washington University in St. Louis). If you type www.washington.edu in your browser, you would be taken to the University of Washington Web site.

You can also read one of the college search books listed in the appendix.

Furthermore, to enroll in an honors program at this university, students must write a thesis and present an oral defense of that thesis, similar to what Ph.D. candidates are required to do, although not original research, as is often required for doctorates.

As you can see, the curricula for these two colleges is fairly similar in that both will require 10 or more courses specifically in biology as well as three or more science or math courses. In general, these colleges are typical of the course requirements, although comparing some can be difficult because some colleges are on the semester schedule; others are on the quarter system; some use credit hours; some use units and define the term locally; some offer a greater variety of choice in sciences and other electives; and others limit the number and type of electives.

Minor in Biological Sciences

Many colleges and universities offer students the chance to major in one discipline and minor in another. Essentially, that means you are choosing one primary area of study as well as a secondary specialty. This will appear on your transcript when you graduate.

To minor in bio, students are usually required to take the same introductory courses required of majors, including the lab course, a course in genetics, and three other upper-level biology courses. In addition, of course, you would have to take all of the courses required of the other department in which you are majoring. Although that may require a large commitment of time, many students do so successfully.

If you are considering majoring in a different subject area and minoring in biology, you should speak with an advisor to make sure it is possible at the college you are attending and that you will be able to coordinate the courses easily. Because of the time demands of biology—in particular, the time required for lab courses—some colleges do not permit a minor in bio, especially if the major is in another course requiring lab courses. In addition, it might be impossible to take the required courses in the allotted time because not all courses are offered each semester.

Minors in Other Departments and Double Majors

Many colleges also permit biology majors to minor in another discipline or to double-major in two areas, one of which can be biology. Often the two fields are related, such as with chemistry or mathematics. But indeed, students have combined biology with such diverse areas as foreign languages, music, and fine arts.

Because of the inherent time commitment required, doing a double major in engineering is difficult. But with careful planning and guidance, this also can be accomplished. The university featured earlier, like many others, does not permit students to do a double major (or a minor) in two of the biology fields it offers. In other universities, it may be possible to double major in two bio fields, although probably not recommended.

College Rankings

Ranking colleges is a popular pastime about which I have very strong negative feelings. To me, rankings are of little value to students. I say that for a number of reasons: (1) the rankings are quite subjective; (2) a high ranking in one major (or even one area of biology) does not necessarily mean a similar ranking in another major or area; (3) you can find little difference between, say a ranking of 25 and 30; and (4) a college that is excellent for one student might be subpar for another. Certainly, you would agree that there is no real difference between colleges ranked as numbers one and two. If you are the kind of student that thrives in a small college atmosphere, but you attend a more highly ranked college that is large, was that a good choice for you? Maybe not. Just because a college is ranked high one year—just before you start your freshman year—is there any guarantee that by your senior year it will still be ranked highly? And which is more important, a high ranking based on strong faculty and research, even though in your first two years you will be taking introductory courses, or a high ranking when you're a senior and have access to some of these great faculty members?

Colleges Offering Biology Programs

Although there are many reasons to disregard rankings, I do believe it is essential to look at lists of colleges to determine whether or not you have a chance of getting accepted. The last thing you want is to find yourself not accepted at any college.

With that in mind, I offer the following lists of colleges to help you get a leg up on which colleges to apply to. I have provided a partial list of colleges that offer excellent biology programs, broken up by whether they are highly selective (admit under 50 percent of applicants) or less selective (admit more than 75 precent of applicants) and listed in alphabetical order (not ranked). Because of the number of colleges offering biology as a major, this list is just a sample. For more information about them and other colleges, I recommend you use one of the excellent handbooks available, listed in the Appendix.

BIOLOGY*

Highly Selective

Amherst College (MA)

Bowdoin College (ME)

Brandeis College (MA)

Brown University (RI)

California Institute of Technology (CA)

California, University of—Berkeley (CA)

California, University of—Los Angeles (CA)

Columbia University (NY)

Cornell University (NY)

Duke University (NC)

Emory University (GA)

Georgetown University (DC)

Harvard University (MA)

Harvey Mudd College (CA)

Johns Hopkins University (MD)

Lehigh University (PA)

Massachusetts Institute of Technology (MA)

New York University (NY)

North Carolina, University of—Chapel Hill (NC)

Northwestern University (IL)

Princeton University (NJ)

Reed College (OR)

Rice University (TX)

Stanford University (CA)

Texas, University of—Austin (TX)

University of Southern California (CA)

Vanderbilt University (TN)

Virginia, University of (VA)

Washington University (MO)

Yale University (CT)

Less Selective

Arcadia (PA)

Berea (KY)

Brooklyn College (NY)

California Polytechnic State University (CA)

College of Charleston (SC)

East Stroudsburg (PA)

Eastern Connecticut (CT)

Eastern Oregon (OR)

Fitchburg (MA)

Heidelberg (OH)

Lewis-Clark (ID)

Lycoming (PA)

Lynchburg (VA)

North Carolina, University of—Wilmington (NC)

Northern Michigan (MI)

Rhode Island College (RI)

Rider College (NJ)

Tougaloo (MS)

West Chester (PA)

Wyoming, University of (WY)

BIOCHEMISTRY*

Highly Selective

Barnard (NY)

Brandeis (MA)

California, University of—Berkeley (CA)

California, University of—Los Angeles (CA)

Columbia University (NY)

Cornell University (NY)

Georgia, University of (GA)

Harvard University (MA)

Iowa, University of (IA)

Massachusetts Institute of Technology (MA)

Miami, University of (FL)

Pennsylvania, University of (PA)

Princeton University (NJ)

Rice University (TX)

Rutgers University (NJ)

Less Selective

California State University—Channel Islands (CA)

California State University—Fullerton (CA)

Framingham (MA)

Nevada, University of—Reno (NV)

Northern Illinois (IL)

Ohio Northern (OH)

Oregon State (OR)

Sacred Heart (CT)

Temple (PA)

ZOOLOGY*

Highly Selective

California, University of—Berkeley (CA)

Cornell University (NY)

Florida, University of (FL)

Miami University (OH)

Michigan, University of (MI)

North Carolina, University of—Chapel Hill (NC)

Pennsylvania State University (PA)

Wisconsin, University of (WI)

Less Selective

California Polytechnic State University (CA)

Colorado State University (CO)

Eastern Illinois (IL)

Howard (DC)

Louisiana State (LA)

Montana, University of (MT)

Oregon State (OR)

San Jose State (CA)

Southern Illinois (IL)

Weber State (UT)

*I compiled these lists with the help of a few resources: Rugg, Frederick E., *Rugg's Recommendations on the Colleges*, 2004; The College Board, *The College Handbook*, 2004; *Peterson's Four-Year Colleges*, Thomson Peterson's, 2004.

Entrance Requirements

Before starting your college biology program—whether you are seeking either a B.A. or B.S. degree—you must have completed a specific number of courses in high school or prep school. Following are the minimums and recommended numbers of required years of precollege study.

Precollege Courses				
	Bachelor of Arts Degree		**Bachelor of Science Degree**	
	Required	Recommended	Required	Recommended
English	4 years	4 years	4 years	4 years
Social Studies	3 years	3 years	4 years	4 years
Math*	3 years	3 years	4 years	5 years
Lab Science**	2 years	2 years	3 years	3 years
Foreign Language	2 years	2 years	3 years	3 years
Academic Electives	3 years	3 years	5 years	4 years

* selected from algebra I, algebra II, geometry, trigonometry, analytic geometry, functions, math analysis, calculus

** selected from biology, chemistry, physics or other advanced lab science

Skills and Abilities Required to Succeed in This Major

It should come with little surprise that success in biology requires strong quantitative and analytical skills. Keep in mind, however, that much of this is learned through coursework and study. It's not something you already know! It's helpful, of course, to have an aptitude for science and to be analytical in your approach to your studies. But you should not rule out a career in biology, even if you found some of the coursework in high school challenging. Some of our greatest scientists and mathematicians—Albert Einstein, to name one—struggled through their courses in fields in which they later excelled.

That said, it does help to have some particular skills in order to succeed as a biology major and, later on, as a professional. Of course, practical knowledge of the fundamentals of biology and other technical areas, such as chemistry and math, is important, and much of that you can pick up in high school. But in addition, there are some other areas in which you should feel comfortable. For example, you should have good oral and written communication skills since many positions in the bio field require writing articles and speaking to individuals as well as to small and large groups. You could be working in the field of public health, for example, where dealing with the public is a major part of your job. Or you could be writing up your experiments and presenting papers on them, so being able to write clearly will help you. Again, writing is a skill you can learn through practice and study. But you should know going in that you will likely do a lot of writing if you stay in the biology field.

You should feel comfortable working with data and information because analysis and interpretation are key parts of being a scientist. And you should probably feel comfortable working with scientific equipment if you intend to conduct research. Again, these can both be learned in high school and advanced studies.

Apart from the specific skills you need to succeed, there are some other areas where specific abilities can help when you graduate with a degree in biology.

First of all, you should have a basic curiosity about the world. Much of scientific research and work requires that you think about how things work or how they are. And being creative in your thinking will also help you "think outside the box," so you don't just accept things as they are.

Secondly, since researchers, writers, and scientists do much of their work alone—designing studies, analyzing data, or writing up results— the ability to work independently will help you. At the same time, you will want to have the ability to work as part of a team, because rarely are studies done by just one person.

Wrap Up

Now that you know a little about what it will be like to be a biology major and what might be required of you, we will talk about how to choose a college and how to pay for it. We will provide insight into what admission officers are looking for in college admission applications. Admissions professionals repeatedly say that the most important part of a college entrance application is the transcript. For some colleges, that one factor will make or break the decision. So it will be important for you to look at the courses you took with a critical eye. Did you challenge yourself? Will that reflect in your transcript?

We'll also discuss test scores, letters of recommendation, extracurricular activities, and the personal statement to give you an idea of how they affect the decision of whether or not you are admitted.

In the next chapter, we talk about how you can afford to go to the college of your choice even if your family's resources are limited. We demonstrate that no student, regardless of ability to pay, will be denied the opportunity to attend. Yes, we understand and point out that a great deal of need-based financial aid is in the form of loans that students—and their families—have to pay back later. But we make the clear point that getting a college education is well worth the financial risk.

Chapter 2

Choosing a College for Biology Majors

Choosing the right college implies that among the more than 3,000 colleges and universities in the United States there is a single, magical campus that will meet your needs better than any other institution. This is simply not true. For any single student there are several colleges that will enable you to reach your academic, personal, and social goals. The question is one of finding the right match.

To Parents:

The most frightening words admission officers hear parents say are "We are applying to your college." The fact is, it's not your turn. It's your child's education we are concerned about now. On every parent's list of schools they would choose for their son or daughter are their alma maters and the schools that turned them down. As difficult as this may be, this is the opportunity to begin recognizing your child as an individual separate from you—nurtured and loved by you—but now facing a world unlike the one in which you grew up and one very likely to have different needs.

Begin with an honest conversation. Set the ground rules; you know you have some. They often include how much money you can contribute, what distance is too far from home, and which schools are on and off your acceptable list.

Be a mirror. Your child will be looking at a range of schools. When she speaks of attending a large university, ask "Remember when you took that large class? Was that the kind of experience that brings out the best in you?" Or in questioning his interest in a technical school specializing in science, you might say, "You often say that high school is too confining. Does that have anything to do with the limited kinds of experiences available?"

Last, be a true support for your child. Divide up the many complicated tasks involved in the admission process. Some are perfectly appropriate for parents, such as finding out about deadlines, arranging for visits, and helping gather information. But then be certain to get out of the way so that your child can handle those he or she must do.

To Students:

Be organized. Meeting deadlines, writing essays, preparing for and taking standardized tests, visiting campuses, and being the best high school student you can be, all require that you be organized. Keep calendars, make files, use online organizers, post reminders on your bathroom mirror—do what works for you. And remember, if you aren't organized, you are inviting your parents to organize you!

Be honest with yourself. Unlike much of what happens in high school, this is not a time to compare yourself with others. Take a careful assessment of your needs, strengths, and dreams. And then make decisions that fit you, not only based on who you are now, but also on who you hope to be. It is an all-too-common mistake for students to choose colleges based on the views of their friends, parents, siblings, or last year's seniors. Have the courage to forge your own path and consider colleges that meet your needs, even if that means being the first in your family or school to apply to a particular college.

Avoid the designer-label trap. Prestige and quality are not always found in the same institution. In general, look for those elements in a college that will most directly support who you are as a student. Keep an eye on your goal to major in either a general biology program or a specific field within that major. Unless you are absolutely, positively sure of the specific field you want to pursue, be sure to keep an open mind about some of the others within the field of biology out there.

Most important, remember that you are in charge. Although you might believe you have little control, the fact is that most of the power in this process resides with you. You are responsible for the quality of your schoolwork and the level of effort you devote to your college search and application. Those on the other side of the table (that is, the admission officers) make decisions based upon what you present to them. Give them your best.

What Admission Officers Look For

Ask any admission officer what three elements are the most important in the admission application, and the answer will likely be "courses, courses, and courses." The admission officer's job is to bring to the campus those students the faculty most want to teach. Although it certainly doesn't always hold true, the best measure of a student's potential in college is his or her performance in the high school classroom.

THE TRANSCRIPT

Students say their transcripts are not a true reflection of their abilities, that they are just pieces of paper providing only one dimension of their accomplishments. Here's an important tip: that's *not* what admission officers see.

Most admission officers read the transcript as a dynamic, multidimensional document. It speaks about your level of motivation: have you challenged the available curriculum, or taken the easiest path through school? Have you pushed yourself to take an advanced placement (AP) course in biology with the risk of not doing as well as you might have in a regular bio class? Have you demonstrated range, depth, and breadth in the other courses you've taken, in addition to biology? Is there evidence of a willingness to try new things? Perhaps, most importantly, is there a sense of trend? Are you maturing, gaining strength in the upper grades or in courses not related to biology? Or are you taking it easy knowing you have already achieved a certain level of accomplishment?

The transcript is like a relief map of your high school experience.

Note for home-schooled students: If you are home-schooled, and indeed, it is a growing trend, there are very few rules about how colleges handle admission decisions with regard to transcripts. In fact, because each college receives so few applicants who are home-schooled, they vary from year to year and even from student to student. If you took any form of standardized achievement test (for example, state subject tests, Advanced Placement, SAT II), those scores weigh heavily in lieu of grades. If not, colleges rely more heavily on the SAT I or ACT, as well as letters of recommendation and personal statements.

TEST SCORES

Test scores might cause the most anxiety for college applicants, as well as to their parents. More than one million students take the SAT or ACT every year as a requirement for college admission. Many applying to more selective colleges and universities also take the SAT II in specific subjects.

What do admission officers look for when reading your test scores?

Obviously, acceptable ranges vary from college to college. But for the most part, test scores are used as one element of consideration, often to raise questions or to confirm the obvious. A student with high test scores but mediocre grades can raise questions about motivation. Is the student bright, but lazy? If so, the admission officer must be satisfied that this will not be an impediment to college work.

Conversely, the student with very high grades and low test scores raises questions such as how demanding was the student's course load? Is there grade inflation at the school? Or is there a language barrier or learning disability?

Your test scores give one more clue to interpreting your record—another way to add both dimension and detail to the map your transcript represents.

It's important to remember when you are considering your test scores that regardless of the actual scores, there *will* be a college that will accept you into its program. Obviously the higher your scores, the more choices you will have. But you should not be dissuaded from applying to a particular college just because your standardized test scores were not in the range that college lists in their admissions literature. Ranges shown are averages, not absolutes. And indeed, the college handbooks or literature often cite the middle 50 percent of student test scores, not the highest and lowest scores.

Many students take the SAT or ACT more than once. More often than not the scores are just about the same, although simply because of having gained more experience, the later score is a bit higher. However, if the scores are quite different, regardless of whether it was the first or second score, it would be helpful for you to explain to the college why. It may be, for example, that you were sick for one of the tests, or that you prepared more thoroughly for one. You can use your personal statement to explain the difference. Generally you are required to submit both scores to the college.

THE ESSAY OR PERSONAL STATEMENT

The personal essay allows each applicant to help admission officers read the map more accurately. In addition to speaking of your goals, dreams, and expectations, you can explain any gaps or changes in your record in your essay. The essay is your chance to take some control in the admissions process, to thoughtfully and persuasively make your own case.

Admission officers look for writing ability, certainly. But they also look for originality and logic, to gain a fuller sense of your abilities and aspirations. The most effective essays convey an authentic voice, something that is not easily explained, but something admission officers appreciate and recognize readily. The authentic voice doesn't come from trying to satisfy or impress the reader with big words you are not comfortable using or with saying the obvious. Nor is it seen in an essay overly screened and edited by your counselors or parents. It comes through when students convey a true essence of personality and give the reader a deeper understanding of their individual strengths.

Although voice in an essay is important, don't overlook the more mundane aspects, such as good grammar and spelling. That is where your parents and advisors can help.

EXTRACURRICULAR ACTIVITIES

Most applications ask you to list your accomplishments and extracurricular activities. Some students obsess about these and join every activity possible, especially in their senior year. These students are missing the point. The last reason to do those things is to improve the look of your application—that screams of superficiality. Admission officers are more interested in a depth of involvement borne from your true interests. A person with a singular interest, pursued with passion, is far more appealing than one who touches lightly on many. And just because you are applying to be a biology major does not mean you should have been involved solely with related activities. Colleges look for well-rounded people, not just specialists. Of course, be sure to list and explain those bio-related pursuits. Be sure you also include activities with which you were extremely involved earlier in your life, not necessarily those you participated in during your later years in high school. If you were in scouting or 4-H for most of your childhood, for example, but ended your involvement when you got to high school, you might consider including them. But remember that colleges are not looking for the longest list, only those activities that were significant for you.

RECOMMENDATIONS

For recommendations, admission officers want to hear from a few people who know you well and can write convincingly about your abilities, not a long list of important people with whom you've had limited interaction. You need not be described as a paragon of virtue or as the next Nobel Prize winner for your original research in biology. A compelling recommendation might come from a teacher who gave you a "B" but who speaks of your determination and tenacity in pursuing a difficult subject. That teacher can be in the biology department or not, although if you have been working on a bio-related project in school or in your community, it would be helpful for your supervisor or advisor on that project to write a letter for you. If you worked after school, even in a nonbiology-related job, a letter of recommendation from your supervisor or employer might demonstrate the kind of stick-to-itiveness and willingness to take on responsibility that mean a great deal to the admissions committee. Perhaps even more so than a letter from your biology teacher who can only talk about how you got good grades in class but who didn't know much more about you.

   Important: It is advisable that before asking someone to write a letter of recommendation, especially if you are applying to a highly selective college, you speak to that person about what the letter will say. If you get a sense that he or she does not know you well or that the letter will be somewhat negative, you should consider asking someone else.

It's certainly okay for the person to say that you started off weakly but grew a great deal and by the end of your class or employment had demonstrated excellence. That, in fact, shines quite well on admissions applications. But unless the writer can be positive about your ability and/or drive, it's best to find a different person.

A Final Point About Admission

Most admission officers are looking for a reason to admit you, not to keep you out. If you look at your application, transcript, test scores, recommendations, and personal essay as instruments over which you have control, you can use them to build a clear and convincing argument.

Paying for the College of Your Choice

The first thing you should do is say to yourself over and over that you will *not* rule out any college or university because of the cost. The second thing you should do is talk about paying for college with your parents and say the same thing, "do *not* rule out any college or university because of the cost."

I say this very simply because of financial aid and the concept of net cost, not sticker price. It is very possible—and is often the case—that the out-of-pocket costs to you and your family will be less at a high-price college than at a lower cost state-supported university. It is all based on the availability of need-based aid, your family's financial strength, and whether or not the college uses merit-based aid (scholarships and grants) to lure you to that school.

Access and Choice

The foundation of all student financial aid programs are the two concepts of access and choice. They usually go hand-in-hand and essentially say that no students will be denied the opportunity to go to their college of choice based on their inability to pay. It's simple to state, but of course, much more difficult to put into practice and explain. To explain requires a little bit of knowledge about how the financial aid system works.

First, our society has put aside a great deal of money to help students who otherwise would not be able to attend the college of their choice.

And when I say a great deal of money, I'm talking about more than $122 *billion* dollars in just the 2003–2004 year. That extraordinary amount comes from several sources, including the federal government, state governments, colleges and universities themselves, foundations, and private agencies.

Most of that money is based on the family's need, which is tied into the cost of attendance. By that I mean, if you want to attend your local state college because you feel it would be the right match for you, and the college costs $11,354 (which just happens to be the average total charge for public, four-year colleges for 2004–2005 according to The College Board annual survey), but you can afford to pay only $8,000, your need is the difference, or $3,354. It will be up to the college to use its funds, money from the federal and state governments, and money from other sources to fill that need; otherwise you won't attend. The good news is that for the most part, the college will, in fact, come up with a way for you to get the needed funds.

Similarly, if you decide you want to attend a four-year private college out of town that costs $27,516 (the average total charge for 2004–2005 at four-year private colleges, according to The College Board annual survey), your "need" is the difference, or $19,516. If you don't get that amount in some form of financial assistance, you won't be able to attend. It's as simple as that. The whole point of choice is that just because a college costs more doesn't mean you can afford any more. A graphic description of this principle is provided in the table below.

In order for you to attend College 1, you'll need a little more than $3,000; for College 2, you need more than $19,000; and for College 3, you need more than $25,000. If you don't get those amounts, you won't attend those colleges.

	College 1 (Public)	College 2 (Private)	College 3 (Private)
Cost of Attendance	$11,354	$27,516	$33,280
Expected Family Contribution (EFC)	$8,000	$8,000	$8,000
Demonstrated Need	$3,354	$19,516	$25,280

DETERMINING NEED

Wouldn't it be nice if all we had to do was say, "Hey, I need $25,000 to attend College 3 this year. Can I have it?" Obviously it doesn't work quite so easily. And here's where the financial aid application process comes in. There are complex formulas used to determine your family's ability to pay. When you apply for aid, you are, in effect, providing the information needed.

You complete the information requested on the FAFSA (Free Application for Federal Student Aid) and, if appropriate, the PROFILE (used by many private colleges), submit it (this can be done on the Web), and out comes a figure called the Expected Family Contribution (EFC). That is the figure used in the preceding table.

Then your demonstrated need is simply the difference between the total cost of attendance at that particular college and your EFC.

COST OF ATTENDANCE

The cost of attendance can be easily seen in the brochures and catalogs available online, in the literature sent to you, or in one of the many books listing the costs. What is included are

◆ Tuition

◆ Required fees

◆ Room and board (average if not living in campus housing)

◆ Books and supplies

◆ Transportation

◆ Other personal and miscellaneous expenses

These costs are what a student will need to attend that college for one year (actually, for the 9-month period). Summer programs are not usually included, although students who choose to attend can receive additional financial aid to help pay for them, and costs that are unique to particular students (those with disabilities, for example, or those who live farther away and, therefore, need more money to get home for vacations), can have their budgets increased by the financial aid office (sorry, parking tickets and the high cost of pizza delivery are not

College	Tuition/Fees (Biology)	Room/Board/ Other expenses	Total Charge
Boston University	$30,402	$11,898	$42,300
Harvard	$30,620	$13,230	$43,850
Ohio State	$7,479	$11,121	$18,600
Carnegie Mellon	$30,650	$11,320	$41,970
UCLA	$6,028	$15,330	$21,358
University of Illinois	$10,280	$8,768	$19,048
Rice	$19,670	$11,368	$31,038
Stanford	$28923	$12,658	$41,581
University of Texas	$5,314	$10,634	$15,948

included). Room and board expenses for those living off campus in private houses or apartments usually have a maximum budget set, which is based on the average in that community. Financial aid offices usually do surveys to make those determinations.

For books and supplies, the budgets will include fees required of biology majors since often there are lab fees over and above the regular student fees. In fact, at the University of Illinois, they show a required fee for bio majors of $2,314, over and above the required tuition and fees.

Above are the estimated budgets for a number of colleges and universities that offer programs in biology. For state colleges, the tuition and fees figure is for residents of that state.

Types of Financial Aid

Since we already discussed the more than $122 billion in financial aid, we should point out a few facts about the types of aid that are awarded.

You can receive financial aid in three ways: it can be given to you as "free money" (in the form of grants or scholarships); you can borrow it (loans); or you can earn it (through working).

The fact is, as you probably already know, not all the aid given to students is free. But of the total amount of aid awarded to undergraduate students, just under half (44 percent) was given in the form of grants and scholarships. And just over 5 percent was given to students in the form of tax breaks (which amounts to free money since taxes were lowered). One percent was earned through the Federal College Work Study program, and the rest, (just under 50 percent) was loaned to students for them to pay back after they graduate—usually at lower interest rates than other loans. Loans, of course, only help you to defray the costs since you will ultimately be paying them back. But the bottom line is that half of the total cost of education was paid for through grants, scholarships, and lower taxes, leaving you with more money in your pocket. So although the costs to attend college appear to be close to $30,000 annually for private colleges, on average, and $11,000 annually for state colleges, that's not really what some 70 percent of the student population are paying. That's where net cost comes in.

Net Cost versus Sticker Price

The preceding table shows the sticker price—that is, the total amount that will be charged. But the question arises, "How much will you pay?"

As we said earlier, with more than $122 billion in financial aid available, it's likely that you won't be paying the full retail price, but, rather, a lower amount. And in some cases, a significantly lower amount. If your college charges you the average private four-year cost of $27,500, and you qualify for $20,000 in financial aid, about half of that will be in the form of loans, and then you're really only paying $17,500 out of pocket. And if you qualify for even more aid because your family's resources are less, or if you win a merit-based scholarship or grant from an outside agency, you would wind up paying much less.

We can't give you hard data on the actual amounts you'll be paying, but we can refer you to several sources of information and Web sites that can help you calculate your Expected Family Contribution so that you can determine your need. From there, you can estimate your net cost.

Is It Worth It?

Given that the costs of going to college, as we've already shown, range from about $16,000 to more than $40,000 per year (and likely to increase each year), we would be remiss if we didn't ask the burning question, "Is it worth that kind of cost to go to college?"

To answer that question, we need to look at two areas. The first is financial, and the question we must ask is, "How much more will you earn if you go to college?" We've done the research for you, and according to The College Board's report, *Education Pays*, the average earnings for people with just a high school diploma was $30,800 per year in 2003. For those who earned a bachelor's degree, the average earnings in 2003 was $49,900, or 62 percent more than for the high school graduate. The figures are even more dramatic for those with masters and doctorate degrees.

If we look at earnings over a lifetime, we see that the cumulative earnings of high school graduates will be about $1 million in today's dollars; for college grads, that number is $1.73 million. And even accounting for the cost of paying for college and the lost wages while attending those 4 or 5 years, by age 33, the typical college graduate who enrolled at age 18 will catch up to the high school grad who did not go on to college. Clearly, from just a financial point of view, attending college is well worth it, even when you factor in the cost of attendance and lost wages.

The second question has to do with some of the other benefits of going to college, both to you and to society. Here again the data are conclusive. The qualify of life for college graduates is clearly better, with college grads reporting that they are in better health, have less incidence of poverty, lower employment rates, and lower incarceration rates. The wonderful thing is that this benefit gets passed on to future generations since children of college graduates go on to college at a higher rate than children of parents who did not go to college.

It is also interesting to look at whether society as a whole benefits by you going to college. In fact, this is also true. Since they earn more than high school graduates, college grads clearly contribute more in taxes. They also cost society less because they don't need to take advantage of as many federal and state social programs, such as aid to families with dependent children, food programs, unemployment compensation, or Medicaid. And on a strictly nonfinancial level, there are other benefits. College graduates even smoke less than those who did not go to college; they tend to volunteer their time more; they vote at higher rates than noncollege grads; and they even donate blood more.

Regardless of whether you continue your studies in biology or any other field, by going on to college, you will have bettered your life enormously and contributed more to society.

Private Scholarships and Scholarship Search Firms

Although we have not discussed types of free money in any depth, suffice it to say that there are government grants, institutional grants, and grants from foundations, individuals, and organizations. Most are based strictly on need; some are based on merit; and some are a combination of the two. When you apply for financial aid, you are automatically applying for need-based government and institutional grants. In addition, many institutions will use merit-based grants (also called scholarships) to encourage you to select that college, concerned that you might choose to attend elsewhere. If you have financial need, the merit-based grant or scholarship will be included in your award and will likely mean you have to borrow or work less. If you do not qualify for need-based aid, that scholarship will offset the cost your parents will have to shell out.

Private scholarships you receive from outside organizations also figure into your award, and you must apply for them separately. Sending in your financial aid application does not mean you've applied for a private scholarship, except those that the college itself awards. Many organizations award money for students to attend college. These can be local groups (service groups such as Rotary and the local Lions club or your high school scholarship committee), your parents' employer, international corporations, or foundations. Sometimes the amounts can be quite significant; sometimes just a few hundred dollars. But you must apply for them separately, and often the competition is staggering. You must decide whether it will be worth the effort to complete the application or, instead, focus your energy on raising your grades and/or test scores. Obviously the more money that is at stake, the lower the odds of you winning the competition. Your best bet is to look at local organizations rather than national or international ones.

Scholarship search firms are private for-profit companies that often promise you a number of scholarships for which you are eligible. The operative words here are "for which you are eligible." You are not guaranteed that you will receive any, just that you are eligible to apply. These firms will charge you money to find sources of scholarships and, to be blunt, my advice to you is that you should avoid any scholarship search firm that charges you a fee. Even the Federal Trade Commission

(FTC) has issued a warning for students and their families about these scholarship search firms. In the Appendix are several Web sites on which you can access a free scholarship search, including www.collegeboard. com, www.finaid.org, and www.fastweb.com.

Part of the lure from scholarship search firms is the notion that thousands of scholarships go unused. Frankly, that is hogwash. The bulk of these are scholarships that must be used at specific colleges by individuals who meet very specific criteria. For the most part, the colleges themselves award these scholarships. Many of the other scholarships listed are federal programs (and some are not even grants but loans). Again, you should avoid any firm that asks you to pay for a scholarship search.

Wrap Up

In this chapter I talked about the admission process and how admission officers consider the strength of your application in their admission decisions. I also demonstrated to you, I hope, that after you are accepted, you can attend the college of your choice regardless of you or your family's ability to pay. Not to belabor my point, but I want to emphasize that the basic rule of financial aid is that no one should be denied the opportunity to attend the college of his or her choice based on money. If you're unclear or uncertain about this premise, I strongly advise you to speak to the financial aid administrator at the college to which you are applying.

In the next chapter I will address some of the possibilities for you after you leave college with your bachelor's degree. Of course, like most of your fellow students, you can go right on to employment, and in Chapter 4 I list many different jobs for which you are qualified with your biology degree. But as an alternative to going out into the working world, you can enroll in an internship, which is somewhat of a cross between school and work. Or, you can go on to graduate school, which I will also discuss in the next chapter. I will explain the various disciplines within the field of biology, the admission application process, and how to pay for graduate school. And I will make it clear, I hope, that decisions you make now are not "forever." There is much time in your life to change your mind and to choose a new direction, even if you have already moved successfully into one field.

Chapter 3

Internships and Attending Graduate School

With your bachelor's degree in biology in hand, you're well-armed to enter the wonderful world of employment and well-prepared to find a challenging, well-paying job. In the next chapter, we'll discuss some interesting job possibilities for which you are qualified with your undergraduate degree in the biological sciences. Then we'll talk about jobs for which you need an advanced degree, either a master's or doctorate. In Chapter 5 we'll provide you with tips and guidance to help you in your job search, including tips on preparing your resume, interviewing techniques, networking, and making the most of your contacts.

In this chapter, however, we want to talk to those of you who do *not* want to go right into the working world, but rather, who are interested in either continuing your education—because there are job possibilities you want for which you need an advanced degree—or want to continue learning through internships.

I explain what an internship is, how you can apply for one, and point you toward some ways to find organizations that offer them. Then I'll discuss graduate school and show you some of the different specialties you can enter. I'll highlight some graduate programs and list the kinds of courses you'll need to take, just as we did for the undergraduate program. I'll talk about applying to graduate schools so you can see how different the process is from applying to undergraduate school. And I'll talk about how you can finance grad school. It, too, is different for grads than for undergrads so you need to be well aware of that before deciding whether to go on. But let's first talk about internships.

Biology Internships

One of the alternatives to entering the job market either post-undergraduate or during the summers while you are in college is doing an internship. So what exactly is an internship? Essentially, it's a training period for someone just entering the field. During this hopefully brief period, which can range from several weeks to many months, you can get on-the-job experience in the field. You can learn exactly what the biologists and other professionals do in their jobs, not just make assumptions about their work from reading job descriptions. You can often assist them in their work, and depending on the organization, the number of interns, and the person to whom you are assigned, you might get to do highly responsible work. The good part about this is that you are not just left out there to fail or do poor work. You generally receive close supervision and a great deal of training so that your chances of success are maximized.

For the organization, internships enable them to hire capable people who can do some of the needed work but typically at very low (or no) cost. Furthermore, interships enable them to develop a pool of qualified applicants from which they can select if and when a real job opens.

If you think back to your the history lessons, you will remember that throughout most of history professionals, who were usually tradesmen, hired apprentices whom they could teach to assist them in their work and take over the business when they were no longer able to keep up with the workload. Being an intern is quite similar in nature, and it tends to be a win-win for both parties.

Internships are available in just about every field of biology, whether you are interested in ecology, biomedical research, marine biology, zoology, or scores of other areas.

WHY WOULD I WANT TO BE AN INTERN?

The most obvious reason you would choose to be an intern is that you can't find a job in the field you want and that the only way to work in that field is by interning. But there are other compelling reasons for doing an internship. One is the training you will receive. Although as an undergraduate you learned a great deal of biology, you generally did not get to do a lot of the kinds of things you would do when you work as a biologist or at a biology-related job. Supposing, for example, that you had a particularly strong affinity for ecology and environmental causes. You certainly can talk a lot about the science involved. And you might love teaching kids about it. But you might not be qualified to teach professionally, nor are you strongly drawn to getting a graduate degree in education so you can get a teaching certificate. Many internships allow you the chance to actually teach young people about nature and ecology and do not require that you already are a certified teacher. A couple of the people featured in the case studies later in this book were interns before getting full-paying jobs, one of whom actually did teach nature and science in her internship.

A second reason you might consider doing an internship is that it gives you something to do when you really do not know what you want to do professionally. Internships allow you the chance to try out something and work in the field before committing totally to that kind of job. If you take a summer internship, you might decide after the summer that you would prefer a different field of biology. Having completed the internship and then choosing another area would not reflect poorly on you when you did apply for a job; whereas if you moved from field to field in a paid position, employers might question your motivation and, as a result, might not hire you.

A third reason to consider an internship is the notion that after you have demonstrated your ability, you are more likely to be offered a job by the organization for which you worked as an intern. Often that is the case. But you should also be aware that some organizations have policies against such a thing. Still, it can never hurt for future employment possibilities, even if you can't get a job with that organization immediately.

Finally, a fourth reason to do an internship is that you can't find a paying job. This may not be the best of all reasons; it is certainly better for you to do something professional, even as an intern, than to flip burgers at your local fast food place.

WILL I GET PAID?

The quick answer to that is, "maybe." The fact is, you can do some internships that will pay you, as if it were a real job. Of course, even if you are paid, the salary will most likely be lower than if you were hired full time as an employee. Some internships provide housing and food so although you might not have a salary, you also won't have many expenses. (*Note:* You often can get a deferment from paying your student loans while you are an unpaid intern, but you must speak to your lender before making that assumption.)

Some internships are considered "fellowships," particularly for those who have already received a bachelor's degree. Most fellowships pay a small stipend or monthly amount.

And some internships, sadly, are volunteer positions. For those you will have to have a external income source, whether it is a second job during your off hours, money from your parents (as if this period was just a part of your college training), or loans (because you are not a student, you are not eligible for financial aid, so any loan you receive will have to be based on you or your parents' credit).

HOW DO I FIND AN INTERNSHIP?

If you are interested in being an intern, the first thing you should do is investigate the possibilities while you are still in school. Both the biology and the career planning departments will have information about possible internships. Some of these opportunities are highly competitive (even if interns are not paid), so you want to start your search early. If you are thinking of doing an internship in the summer after you graduate, for example, you probably should start your search during the fall term so you have the best selection. There will, however, be many internships available to last-minute lookers, just not the highest paid or most sought after.

A second way to begin your search is by directly contacting some of the biggest companies in the field. For example, if you are interested in doing an internship in the pharmaceutical industry, you can contact one of the large pharmaceutical companies, such as Pfizer, by either calling the American headquarters in New York (they will direct you to the appropriate division) or through the Internet (www.pfizerrdgrad. com). Usually there are listings of possible internship opportunities (as well as job listings), application instructions, and contact information.

You can also use a search engine for "biology internships" and check out the results. The results will lead you to hundreds, or even thousands of possibilities. Although many will be listed within university Web sites, maybe even your own college, they will still link you to organizations that are offering the actual internships. A search using Google yielded more than 400,000 listings.

In addition, there are several job search Web sites that provide links to internships, such as

www.http://paidinterns.com

www.theihs.org/intern

www.BioBums.com

www.Closers.net

www.internship-usa.com/

Important: Because some of these internships are highly competitive, you should apply for them with all the same seriousness as you would a job. You will likely have to send transcripts, write a personal statement, and undergo a personal interview. You should be as well prepared as you can by learning as much as you can about the organization and the work it does, by writing a letter specific to that organization, and by presenting yourself professionally in the interview. In addition to helping you find an internship program, your career planning office can assist you in the application process.

Graduate School Programs in Biology

There are almost as many options for graduate school as there are for undergrads, so you shouldn't feel limited. Assuming you did well enough to complete your bachelor's degree, there will almost definitely be a graduate school willing to accept you into its program.

What's significantly different about grad school, however, is that not as many colleges offer graduate programs in general biology. By the time they finish undergraduate school, most students pick an area in which they want to specialize. That's not to say that you can't continue to take classes in various disciplines. But most graduate students in the biological sciences are specialized. And if you are thinking about teaching biology, particularly at the high school level, you'll likely be entering a master's degree program in education, not biology. If you're thinking about teaching at the college level, you'll probably need to choose an area of specialization since most professors of biology spend a great deal of time doing independent research in addition to their teaching load.

The one teaching job in which it may be beneficial to take a wide range of graduate biology courses or to get a master's degree in general biology is community college instructor. Almost all community college instructors have at least a master's degree (some have Ph.D.s), and most also have a specific area of expertise. But because many of the instructors in community colleges teach lower-level biology, they don't necessarily need to have the advanced knowledge of a specific area within biology.

Graduate School Disciplines

Master's level programs are available in a wide variety of disciplines. One university states that they offer concentrations in

- ◆ Molecular biology

- ◆ Microbiology

- ◆ Bioinformatics and computational biology (BCB)

- ◆ Systematics and evolutionary biology

The university also allows students to choose the program in biological sciences that allows flexibility to specialize in additional areas.

Another leading university offers specialties in

- ◆ Biochemistry, cell and developmental bio

- ◆ Genetics and molecular bio

- Immunology and molecular pathogenesis
- Microbiology and molecular genetics
- Molecular and systems pharmacology
- Neuroscience
- Nutrition and health sciences
- Population biology, ecology, and evolution

And a third, emphasizing the interdisciplinary approach that they say has become an essential feature of modern biomedical science, states that genetics, molecular, biochemical, biophysical, and computational methods are integrated to tackle challenging problems in cellular and developmental biology, genetic regulation, macromolecular structure and function, neurobiology, and physiology.

So you see, applying to a graduate school program in biology is not nearly as straightforward as applying for undergraduate school. Then again, after you already have completed three years or more of biology and are thinking about graduate school, chances are you'll know what each of these disciplines are about and may have already specialized.

Master's degree programs generally require about one year of classes; Ph.D. programs about four years. Many master's degrees require that you write a thesis or research paper, although at some schools you can take a comprehensive exam instead. All Ph.D. programs require that you write an original thesis.

For specific requirements, you should check individual college handbooks and catalogs. But you should be aware that some of the highly selective universities do not offer a master's degree program in biology. They offer only Ph.D. programs.

Many universities have no specific courses required for completion of a master's degree program in general biology. Instead, the curriculum you take will be based on your background, interests, and future career goals. However, colleges usually will want you to take biochemistry I and II, cell biology, and advanced genetics in your course of study, since they serve as prerequisites for a number of other courses and are the base for further study in any of the biological sciences.

Quality Programs and Rankings

Literally hundreds of excellent graduate schools offer biology. Although there is a great deal of emphasis on rankings, I am not a believer in following these rankings, particularly when it comes to selecting a graduate program. For one, this kind of list changes from year to year. If you are in high school now, what good would it do for you to know that in 2005, Stanford University or MIT are the top-ranked programs in molecular biology? Chances are, you won't be attending for at least four or five years. Isn't it quite possible that the rankings will change by then, especially since an important factor in ranking is the prestige of the faculty? If one of the key researchers at a university leaves or retires, certainly a possibility in four or five years, that would affect the rankings a great deal.

As I said when I discussed rankings of undergraduate schools, how can you possibly distinguish between two numbers? Is number 12 any "worse" than number 10? Rankings to me are about as important as popularity contests. And for graduate schools, rankings are even less relevant since there are so many different fields within biology. To say that one school is top ranked in micro does not imply that it is also top-ranked in cellular biology or biochemistry.

That said, when selecting the graduate school you want to attend, you should pay attention to these criteria:

◆ Does it offer my specialty?

◆ Does it have the resources I will need to do my research?

◆ Will I have access to the key professors in my area?

◆ Is the school considered one of the "highly selective" schools?

◆ If so, will my grades and scores be good enough to get accepted?

◆ Is it located in a place I'd want to live for several years?

Selecting the right graduate school is not that different than selecting the right undergraduate school. You have to take into account many factors, not just rankings.

Following is a list of universities, in no particular order, that offer graduate programs in most areas of biology and are generally considered highly selective. Although some on the list are universities you would expect to be there, Stanford, MIT, Harvard, and so on, others may surprise you. For example, the first one on this list, University of Wisconsin, has an extremely strong program in microbiology and quality programs in several other areas of biology.

SELECTIVE BIOLOGY GRADUATE SCHOOLS

University of Wisconsin—Madison

Stanford University

University of California—San Diego

University of Pennsylvania

Washington University

Massachusetts Institute of Technology

University of California—San Francisco

New York University

Carnegie Mellon University

University of California—Berkeley

Columbia University

Johns Hopkins University

California Institute Technology

University of North Carolina—Chapel Hill

Yale University

Harvard University

Vanderbilt University

University of Alabama—Birmingham

University of Michigan

Duke University

University of California—Los Angeles

University of Colorado

Ohio State University

University of Michigan

State University of New York—Stony Brook

Rutgers University

University of Texas

Cornell University

University of Washington

University of Chicago

University of California—Santa Cruz

Brandeis University

University of California—Davis

Northwestern University

Rockefeller University

University of Iowa

University of Southern California

Oregon State University

University of Minnesota

Univeristy of Illinois at Urbana—Champaign

HIGHLY RANKED GRADUATE SCHOOLS

The following is a list of a few of the top graduate schools broken down into a few different areas of biology. These rankings are from *U.S. News & World Report* for 2002. Although the same three or four colleges appear repeatedly, the colleges previously listed are also ranked quite highly.

Biological Sciences

Stanford University

MIT

Harvard University

Biochemistry

Harvard University

Stanford University

University of California, San Francisco

Cell Biology

Harvard University

Stanford University

University of California, San Francisco

Yale University

Microbiology

Harvard University

Stanford University

University of Wisconsin

Molecular Biology

Harvard University

Stanford University

MIT

Admission to Grad School

Applying for admission to graduate school is not unlike that of applying to college. You go through pretty much the same selection process to find the right school, the one with the program you want and also one that will accept you; you fill out the application forms; you take a standardized test (the Graduate Record Exam, or GRE) and have your scores sent to the schools selected; you write a personal statement explaining why you want to study at that school and what qualifies you for admission; you get professors, advisors, and supervisors to write letters of recommendation saying you walk on water; you submit official transcripts from *all* the colleges you attended (even if you only took one course there in a summer program); and, of course, you send in your application fee (usually $50 or less).

You should note that some schools waive the application fee for students who apply online, so be sure to check that out—particularly if you're applying to several schools since the fees can add up quickly.

But what's different about applying to graduate school is that there is no common form like for undergraduate school, which means a lot more paperwork or online entering of your information.

For information about the Graduate Record Examination (GRE), write to:
GRE
Educational Testing Service (ETS)
P.O. Box 6000
Princeton, New Jersey 08541-6000.
Or you can check them out at www.gre.org.

Important: When applying to some graduate programs, you apply directly to the biological sciences division, not to the university admission office. Be sure you note carefully where your application is to be submitted.

Words of warning: Graduate programs are just as competitive as undergraduate programs so be sure to work with an advisor on selecting the right programs and schools to apply to. In addition, admission professionals consider you to be a responsible adult. That means they do not tolerate missing information, errors, poorly written personal statements, or letters of recommendation that are anything less than stellar. So be certain you double- and triple-check spelling and grammar when reviewing your statement. And when selecting those people to write a recommendation letter, be sure they know that letters must be glowing and cannot show any weaknesses; otherwise, your admission is jeopardized. Most advisors, professors, and supervisors understand that. But it doesn't hurt to remind them.

Important: Deadlines are just as important for graduate school admission. But they are often quite different in different schools. For example, one grad school requires applications in January for a fall admission, but another doesn't need it until May. Again, be sure to check the school's Web site and literature.

Paying for Graduate School

In many ways, paying for graduate school is similar to paying for an undergraduate program, and in some ways, it is quite different. Let's first look at the similarities:

SIMILARITIES BETWEEN GRAD AND UNDERGRAD

Colleges and universities have the same attitude about admission to graduate school as they do for undergraduate—namely, if a student is admitted, the school has to help work out the financing arrangements.

There is a great deal of financial aid available to help grad students, and the school will work with applicants. That aid can be from various sources, including the Federal and State governments, private foundations, research organizations, lenders, and the institutions themselves.

What that means is that you should not rule out any program just because of the cost.

Financial aid is awarded based both on need and merit. Need is determined by the institution itself using an agreed-upon formula or its own need analysis. The need calculated is based on the cost of attendance minus your expected family contribution. Merit-based aid is awarded based on student scholarship. Sometimes the amount awarded is based on a combination of merit and need.

You apply for financial aid using the same form as you do for undergraduate programs—that is, the FAFSA (www.fafsa.gov) on which you specify the schools to which you want the information sent.

You may also be required to fill out a second form, for example, the PROFILE (www.collegeboard.com) or an institutional form.

Financial aid is available to students who attend part time as well as those going full time. Amounts may be less, especially grant monies, but attending part time may allow you to work and earn a significant amount that you can contribute to your schooling.

While you are attending school at least half time (including graduate school), you are not required to pay off your student loans (you qualify for an in-school deferment). For federal subsidized loans, that means no interest accrues; for federal unsubsidized and private loans, the interest accrues and is added to the principal.

After you complete your schooling, you can consolidate all your student loans into one larger one, even if there were different lenders.

Institutions themselves do the awarding so after you have been accepted for admission and have applied for financial aid, all funding decisions are made by the school.

DIFFERENCES BETWEEN GRAD AND UNDERGRAD

As a graduate student, you are automatically considered to be independent of your parents. Although some programs will continue to ask for parental information (medical school, for example) and may build in an expected contribution from parents, for all federal financial aid, you are considered independent and will not need to provide parental financial information.

Unfortunately, most need-based financial aid for graduate students is in the form of loans. There is very little grant money available, especially from the Federal and State governments.

The maximum loan amounts are significantly higher for graduate students than for undergraduates so it is definitely possible to finance all the costs, which can include summer programs, added expenses for children, higher rents, and so on, by borrowing more.

Fortunately for you, there is a great deal of research money awarded to schools that, in turn, award you funds to attend. Usually it's because you will be working with specific professors on their research, and the funds require that you do the work. Sometimes there are stipends that do not require work, only requiring that you successfully continue in the program and maintain satisfactory academic progress.

Is It Worth It?

In Chapter 2, when discussing the cost of attending college, we posed the question of whether it was worth it. The clear conclusion was a resounding YES. If we look only at financial data, we see that a college graduate will earn significantly more than those with just a high school diploma. The numbers are staggering. On average, almost $50,000 versus just more than $30,000. Over a lifetime, that amounts to $1.7 million for college graduates versus $1 million for those without any college degree. We also showed that the quality of life for college graduates is significantly better for reasons other than financial, and we showed that society as a whole benefits so much more when people attend college. All these things are true even counting in the lost wages and cost of attending college for four or more years.

Okay, but what about graduate school? Is it worth it? We know that at private colleges and universities, the cost of attendance is about $40,000 per year. Since a master's program is usually just one year, that would be the cost. And since the average college graduate earns $50,000 per year, we can see that the expense of attending and wages lost amount to about $90,000.

We know from The College Board's publication *Education Pays: The Benefits of Higher Education for Individuals and Society* (2004) that the average salary for those with a master's degree is $59,500, about

$10,000 more than with just a bachelor's degree. That means, of course, that the average person with a master's degree needs just nine years to make up the costs associated with attending a high-cost, private university. For lower cost public colleges and universities, the costs are made up in significantly less time. So clearly it is worth going on for a master's degree if we just consider the financial benefit.

What about going on for a Ph.D.? That is an altogether different ball of wax. According to The College Board, the average salary for those with a doctorate is $79,400, or about $20,000 more per year than for those with a master's degree. But the additional costs of about $40,000 per year (three additional years), plus the opportunity costs lost ($60,000 per year for three years) means a loss of almost $300,000. Yikes. And with a salary difference of just $20,000, that means about 15 years of working before you break even. Even if you attend a public college where the costs are lower, it will take 10 to 12 years to break even. The financial benefit to getting a Ph.D. is not nearly as clear.

But we really can't consider just the financial benefit. The fact is, having a doctorate puts you in a totally different category and qualifies you for altogether different kinds of jobs. Research biologists, for example, almost all have their doctorates (or are working on them). Pharmaceutical salespeople, on the other hand, very rarely have a Ph.D., and most don't even have a master's degree.

Choices, Choices, Choices

Unless you're one of those people who continues going to school without any break, you're not tied to making a decision about going on to graduate school immediately.

Suppose, for example, you are deeply involved with a research project while in college. You then decide to continue your research as a graduate student and enroll in a master's degree program. Your research reaches a logical conclusion and, like most topics, leads to further questions to be investigated. But just at that time you decide you are not that interested in going further with that research and, in fact, find a job using the knowledge you gained through your studies and research. You can take the job and live happily ever after. Or, after a few years, you might decide to pursue additional research and enroll in a Ph.D. program.

Similarly, let's say you take a job right after you finish college with your bachelor's degree in biology. You're quite happy with your employer and are starting to get interested in moving up the ladder. You apply for various promotions but keep losing out to people with advanced degrees. This is quite common, particularly in scholarly areas like labs. So the simple solution is, you change your mind and go back to graduate school. Very often, people enroll part time while continuing to work full time. Although this is difficult for many people, especially with the rigor and time commitment involved with biology, it is done frequently and successfully. Some employers will even provide time for you to continue your studies and will help pay the costs.

If you graduated from college with a degree in a field other than biology and later decide that you want to go to graduate school in biology, you will have to take a different path. First, you will have to take the courses in biology, chemistry, and math that you didn't take as an undergraduate so that you can demonstrate your ability to succeed in advanced biology courses. A sample curriculum is listed in Chapter 1 and includes at least 10 courses in biology (cell, animal, plant, and microbiology, ecology, and genetics), a year of chemistry, statistics, and two other courses in science. One relatively inexpensive way of doing that is taking courses at the local college on a part-time basis. That will allow you to continue working to pay for the courses. You should keep in mind that in order to qualify for any financial aid, you must be enrolled in a program leading to a degree. So if you are just taking a course here and there, you will not be able to get financial aid, even federal loans.

Second, you will need to take the GRE, just as other students have to do. If you took the test some time ago, you can use those scores. Of course, if you feel that your scores do not reflect your ability, you might want to retake the test, If you do, be sure you prepare just as diligently as you can; otherwise, you might find that your scores are even lower than the earlier ones.

Third, you will have to demonstrate to the graduate school admission officers that you have what it takes to succeed in the program. You will have to explain your motivation and what made you decide to change your current career path. This can all be done on the graduate school application itself since most require a personal statement. On this statement, you should explain what you are currently doing, why it no longer fits your goals, and how it might contribute to your new graduate career.

Helpful advice: Meet with an advisor either at the school you are considering attending or at the school from which you received your bachelor's degree. The advisor can help you formulate a good plan for getting into graduate school and maybe even point you to a biology professor who can give you advice on the field.

The point is, you have choices throughout your life. You don't have to make lifelong decisions straight out of college.

Wrap Up

In this chapter I talked about the possible alternatives available to you should you decide you do not want (or are unable to find) a job. I discussed internships and provided some advice on how to find one, and I talked about going on to graduate school in biology. I also underscored what I said earlier that you have choices in your life and no one decision you make now is final.

In the next chapter, I will provide a list and explanation of various jobs within the field of biology for which you can use all these job searching skills. Some of the jobs will be natural jobs for those who have a degree in biology; some will not be so obvious. Some of the jobs will require an advanced degree; some just a bachelor's degree. I will also provide an approximate salary range to help guide you.

Many people assume that the only jobs for bio majors are either in healthcare or research. The point of this next chapter is to open your mind to some of the different kinds of jobs that exist for people who graduate with a major in biology.

Chapter 4

Career Possibilities

As mentioned in the preceding chapter, a degree in biology will qualify you for many jobs. In this chapter, we will describe some of the possibilities that might not occur to you. Some of the jobs require advanced degrees; some you can get straight out of college with a bachelor's degree (usually a Bachelor of Science). I've specifically omitted doctor, nurse, and most other medical professionals because these positions now usually have their own undergraduate majors (that is, most doctors majored in premed while in college; most nurses majored in nursing, medical laboratory technologists majored in medical technology, and so on). However, many medical professionals did, in fact, major in biology or chemistry as undergraduates before going on to their specialty, particularly those who have been in their profession for a number of years and those who took time off before continuing their graduate education.

Job Descriptions

Many of the job descriptions and earnings estimates given in this chapter were taken from the U.S. Government's Bureau of Labor Statistics. Others were gleaned from actual job listings in newspapers or online. This is by no means an exhaustive list, but rather, a sampling of your options. You can do your own research on job possibilities by going to www.bls.gov and searching under occupations, one of the large newspaper online job listings, or one of the online job search engines (see the Appendix for a list of some of them). For jobs in the Federal government you can check www.usajobs.opm.gov.

HEALTH SCIENTIST ADMINISTRATOR

Health Scientist Administrators develop and implement policies and procedures for research and oversee the scientific review of applications for research training grants. They can work for private research granting agencies or government agencies and must have an advanced degree (Ph.D.) and have done independent research in either human genetics, molecular genetics, molecular biology, computational biology, biochemistry, physical biochemistry, engineering, nanotechnology, mathematics, chemistry, or computer science. Salaries vary with experience but range from about $80,000 to $125,000.

FORESTER

Foresters deal with the management of vegetation, timber, reforestation, and fuels management. They are responsible for the completion of environmental assessment reports and environmental impact statements and the implementation of forestry land management plans. Foresters can work for the government or for companies involved with paper or wood product production. Salaries range from about $50,000 to $100,000, depending on experience and the number of degrees held.

MEDICAL INSTRUMENT TECHNICIAN

Medical instrument technicians work in hospitals and physician's offices and are responsible for ensuring that all the equipment used during procedures function properly. They often operate the equipment and perform the initial analysis of results. Many of these positions are entry-level jobs and, therefore, the salaries range from about $25,000 to $50,000, depending on the level of responsibility.

MEDICAL TECHNOLOGIST

Medical technology is one of the specialty areas within many college biology departments. Graduates, therefore, earn a bachelor's degree in medical technology, not in biology. In a hospital or physician's office lab, med techs usually specialize in either immunohematology, hematology, urinalysis, coagulation, chemistry, microbiology, or serology. They process specimens, prepare reagents, assemble equipment, verify correct instrument operation, and calculate results for a variety of complex tests. One of our case studies in Chapter 6 is the technical director of a hospital laboratory and started as a medical technologist. Salaries range from about $40,000 to $80,000.

PATENT EXAMINER

Patent examiners review patent applications to determine the scope of the protection claimed by an inventor and determine whether or not there are other prior inventions similar to the invention claimed in the patent application. Examiners work for the Federal government in the U.S. Patent Office in the Department of Commerce. A number of specialties exist within biology and biochemistry. Salaries range from about $45,000 to $75,000.

SANITARIAN

Sanitarians are technical experts in the planning, developing, evaluation, and promotion of programs concerned with establishing safe and appropriate facilities. They investigate complaints alleging violations or unsanitary conditions within housing facilities, determine compliance with appropriate licensing standards, and recommend corrective action as needed. They generally work for a public agency (federal, state, or local entity), and the salaries range from about $40,000 to $70,000.

QUARANTINE OFFICER

Quarantine officers work for the U.S. Department of Agriculture to prevent the entry, establishment, and spread of foreign plant pests in the United States and reduce or eliminate outbreaks of certain native pests. They also handle treatment and remedial measures such as disinfection, sterilization, fumigation, cold treatment, hot water treatment, irradiation of regulated articles for plant and animal pests and diseases. Salaries range from about $30,000 to $50,000.

Food Scientist

Food scientists conduct research on bacterial growth and food engineering processes concerning the growth and inactivation of food-borne pathogens and their products. They can work either for regulatory agencies, such as the U.S. Department of Agriculture or for food preparation or food packaging corporations. Salaries vary a great deal depending on experience and education and whether you work in the public or private sector, ranging from about $40,000 to well over $100,000.

Park Guide

Park guides work for the National Park Service or state parks to provide park visitors with first-line information and a variety of interpretive services. They develop and conduct interpretive programs (for example, campfire programs, talks, nature walks, environmental education programs and/or community outreach programs), based on a solid knowledge of natural sciences (for example, biology, geology) and cultural resources (for example, anthropology, archaeology). Many of the jobs are seasonal, but on average, a park guide will make about $20,000 for a 6-month position.

Pharmacologist/Toxologist

Pharmacologists and toxologists plan, implement studies, and evaluate the development of new chemical entities and the improved use of existing drugs. They can work either for the Federal government in the health services area or in the private sector, specifically for pharmaceutical companies. Generally an advanced degree is required, and salaries ranging from $85,000 to $150,000 reflect education and experience.

Forensic Scientist

Forensic scientists are key parts of criminal investigations who work for police departments and other investigatory agencies. Like the characters on the popular TV shows, they examine evidence for the presence of body fluids and other biological material, perform DNA analyses on biological evidence, interpret results of analyses, and testify in court.

Forensic scientists earn from $40,000 to more than $80,000, depending on experience and education.

MEDICAL WRITER

Medical writers write and edit clinical reports, regulatory documents, and both write and edit manuscripts for scientific magazines and journals. They can work for government agencies or in the private sector. Salaries range from about $35,000 to $80,000 or more depending on experience and education.

PUBLIC RELATIONS, PHARMACEUTICALS

Employers in public relations for pharmaceutical and medical equipment companies develop and implement strategic product and corporate public relations programs in the areas of marketed products. They also oversee financial and executive communications and media strategy and stakeholder relations. Public relations specialists with biology backgrounds are well equipped to take on this role. They can move up in the corporate structure so the salary range can be from $40,000 up to a very high level for senior management.

AGRONOMIST

Agronomists are experts in soil management and field-crop production and are involved with the interaction of plants and the environment. They work in both large and small companies, research labs, the Federal government and, of course, in educational settings, either teaching or conducting research. The research they do is applied to developing varieties of crops that grow more efficiently. They use sophisticated research tools and techniques to develop new crop hybrids and varieties. Soil specialists conduct research in everything from the very basic to the applied issues of soil and water management and land use. Agronomists research ways to produce crops and turf and ways to manage soils in the most environmentally friendly way. Bachelor's degrees are required for this career, and Ph.D.s are required for college-level teaching and senior management positions. Agronomists earn approximately $50,000 to $90,000.

ARCHIVIST, CURATOR, AND MUSEUM TECHNICIAN

Archivists, curators, and museum technicians acquire and preserve important artifacts, documents, and other valuable items for permanent storage or display. They work for museums, governments, zoos, botanical gardens, colleges and universities, corporations, and other institutions that require experts to preserve important records, documents, and collectibles. They also describe, catalogue, analyze, exhibit, and maintain valuable objects and collections for the benefit of researchers and the public. Most curators have at least a master's degree, although in smaller museums it's possible to get a curator job with just a bachelor's degree. The pay scale for these positions is fairly low with the entry-level salary starting at about $25,000 and, with experience, going up to about $70,000.

DIETITIAN AND NUTRITIONIST

Dieticians and nutritionists plan food and nutrition programs and supervise the preparation and serving of meals. They help to prevent and treat illnesses by promoting healthy eating habits and recommending dietary modifications, such as the use of less salt for those with high blood pressure or the reduction of fat and sugar intake for those who are overweight. Dietitians manage food service systems for institutions such as hospitals and schools, promote sound eating habits through education, and conduct research. Major areas of practice include clinical, community, management, and consultant dietetics. Most jobs are in hospitals, nursing care facilities, and offices of physicians or other health practitioners. Entry-level jobs earn about $25,000, and more advanced dieticians and nutritionists can earn more than $60,000.

SALES REPRESENTATIVES

The pharmaceutical and medicine manufacturing industry is made up of about 2,500 companies throughout the country. These companies research, develop, and manufacture preparations or finished drugs; biological products, such as serums and vaccines; bulk chemicals and botanicals used in making finished drugs; and diagnostic substances such as pregnancy and blood glucose kits. Sales representatives spend much of their time describing the products to physicians, pharmacists, and health services administrators. Essentially, sales representatives serve as lines of communication between their companies and clients. Most salespeople can do quite well with just a bachelor's degree in biology or chemistry. The average earnings varies greatly but overall, those in pharmaceutical sales earn from $50,000 to well over $100,000.

BIOLOGIST

Biological scientists study living organisms and their relationships to their environment. They research problems dealing with life processes. Most specialize in some area of biology such as zoology (the study of animals) or microbiology (the study of microscopic organisms). Some positions require only bachelor's degrees; some require Ph.D.s. The earnings range accordingly from about $30,000 for entry-level biologists with just a B.S. to well over $100,000 for established biologists. Here is a partial list of biologist positions from the Bureau of Labor Statistics and a brief description of each:

◆ *Aquatic biologists* study microorganisms, plants, and animals living in water. *Marine biologists* study salt water organisms, and *limnologists* study fresh water organisms. Much of the work of marine biology centers on molecular biology, the study of the biochemical processes that take place inside living cells. Marine biologists sometimes are mistakenly called oceanographers, but oceanography is the study of the physical characteristics of oceans and the ocean floor.

◆ *Biochemists* study the chemical composition of living things. They analyze the complex chemical combinations and reactions involved in metabolism, reproduction, growth, and heredity. Biochemists and molecular biologists do most of their work in the field of biotechnology, which involves understanding the complex chemistry of life.

◆ *Botanists* study plants and their environment. Some study all aspects of plant life, including algae, fungi, lichens, mosses, ferns, conifers, and flowering plants; others specialize in areas such as identification and classification of plants, the structure and function of plant parts, the biochemistry of plant processes, the causes and cures of plant diseases, the interaction of plants with other organisms and the environment, and the geological record of plants.

◆ *Microbiologists* investigate the growth and characteristics of microscopic organisms such as bacteria, algae, or fungi. Most microbiologists specialize in environmental, food, agricultural, or industrial microbiology; virology (the study of viruses); or immunology (the study of mechanisms that fight infections). Many microbiologists use biotechnology to advance the knowledge of cell reproduction and human disease.

◆ *Physiologists* study life functions of plants and animals, both in the whole organism and at the cellular or molecular level, under normal and abnormal conditions. Physiologists often specialize in functions such as growth, reproduction, photosynthesis, respiration, or movement, or in the physiology of a certain area or system of the organism.

◆ *Biophysicists* study the application of principles of physics, such as electrical and mechanical energy and related phenomena, to living cells and organisms.

◆ *Zoologists and wildlife biologists* study animals and wildlife—their origins, behavior, diseases, and life processes. Some experiment with live animals in controlled or natural surroundings, and others dissect dead animals in order to study their structure. They also might collect and analyze biological data to determine the environmental effects of current and potential use of land and water areas. Zoologists usually are identified by the animal group studied—ornithologists (birds), mammalogists (mammals), herpetologists (reptiles), and ichthyologists (fish).

◆ *Ecologists* study the relationships among organisms and between organisms and their environments, and the effects of influences such as population size, pollutants, rainfall, temperature, and altitude. Utilizing knowledge of various scientific disciplines, they might collect, study, and report data on the quality of air, food, soil, and water.

ENVIRONMENTAL SCIENTIST

Environmental scientists use their knowledge of the physical makeup and history of the Earth to protect the environment; locate water, mineral, and energy resources; predict future geologic hazards; and offer advice on construction and land-use projects.

Environmental scientists conduct research to identify and abate or eliminate sources of pollutants that affect people, wildlife, and their environments. These workers analyze and report measurements and observations of air, water, soil, and other sources and make recommendations on how best to clean and preserve the environment. Understanding the issues involved in protecting the environment—degradation, conservation, recycling, and replenishment—is central to the work of environmental scientists, who often use their skills and knowledge to design and monitor waste disposal sites, preserve water supplies, and reclaim contaminated land and water to comply with Federal environmental regulations.

FOOD SCIENTIST

Food scientists and technologists usually work in the food processing industry, universities, or the Federal government, and help to meet consumer demand for food products that are healthful, safe, palatable, and convenient. To do this, they use their knowledge of chemistry, physics, engineering, microbiology, biotechnology, and other sciences to develop new or better ways of preserving, processing, packaging, storing, and delivering foods. Some food scientists engage in basic research, discovering new food sources; analyzing food content to determine levels of vitamins, fat, sugar, or protein; or searching for substitutes for harmful or undesirable additives, such as nitrites. They also develop ways to process, preserve, package, or store food according to industry and government regulations. Traditional food processing research into functions involving baking, blanching, canning, drying, evaporation, and pasteurization will continue to be conducted and will find new applications. Other food scientists enforce government regulations, inspecting food processing areas and ensuring that sanitation, safety, quality, and waste management standards are met. Food technologists generally work in product development, applying the findings from food science research to the selection, preservation, processing, packaging, distribution, and use of safe, nutritious, and wholesome food. The earnings for food scientists range from about $30,000 for entry-level bachelor's degree food scientists to close to $100,000 for those with Ph.D.s with considerable experience.

ANIMAL SCIENTIST

Animal scientists work to develop better, more efficient ways of producing and processing meat, poultry, eggs, and milk. Dairy scientists, poultry scientists, animal breeders, and other scientists in related fields study the genetics, nutrition, reproduction, growth, and development of domestic farm animals. Some animal scientists inspect and grade livestock food products, purchase livestock, or work in technical sales or marketing. As extension agents or consultants, animal scientists advise agricultural producers on how to upgrade animal housing facilities properly, lower mortality rates, handle waste matter, or increase production of animal products, such as milk or eggs. The earnings for animal scientists range from about $30,000 for entry-level bachelor's degree food scientists to close to $100,000 for those with Ph.D.s with considerable experience.

MEDICAL LIBRARIAN

Most librarian positions incorporate three aspects of library work: user services, technical services, and administrative services. Still, even librarians specializing in one of these areas have other responsibilities. Librarians in user services, such as reference librarians, work with doctors, medical researchers, and students to help them find the information they need. The job involves analyzing users' needs to determine what information is appropriate, as well as searching for, acquiring, and providing the information. The job also includes an instructional role, such as showing users how to access information. For example, librarians commonly help users navigate the Internet so they can search for relevant information efficiently. Librarians in technical services, such as acquisitions and cataloguing, acquire and prepare materials for use and often do not deal directly with the public. Librarians in administrative services oversee the management and planning of libraries: negotiate contracts for services, materials, and equipment; supervise library employees; perform public-relations and fundraising duties: prepare budgets; and direct activities to ensure that everything functions properly. Medical librarians often have an undergraduate degree in one of the biological sciences and a master's degree in library science. Earnings range from about $35,000 to more than $75,000.

OPTOMETRIST

Optometrists are *doctors of optometry* and provide most primary vision care. They examine people's eyes to diagnose vision problems and eye diseases, and they test patients' visual acuity, depth and color perception, and ability to focus and coordinate the eyes. Optometrists prescribe eyeglasses and contact lenses and provide vision therapy and low-vision rehabilitation. Optometrists analyze test results and develop a treatment plan. They administer drugs to patients to aid in the diagnosis of vision problems and prescribe drugs to treat some eye diseases. Optometrists often provide preoperative and postoperative care to cataract patients, as well as patients who have had laser vision correction or other eye surgery. They also diagnose conditions due to systemic diseases such as diabetes and high blood pressure, referring patients to other health practitioners as needed. Optometrists are often confused with ophthalmologists who have medical degrees. The Doctor of Optometry degree requires the completion of a four-year program at an accredited optometry school and state licensing. The average earnings range from about $60,000 to more than $150,000 per year.

PODIATRIST

Podiatrists are *doctors of podiatric medicine* (DPMs) who diagnose and treat disorders, diseases, and injuries of the foot and lower leg to keep this part of the body working properly. Podiatrists treat corns, calluses, ingrown toenails, bunions, heel spurs, and arch problems; ankle and foot injuries, deformities, and infections; and foot complaints associated with diseases such as diabetes. To treat these problems, podiatrists prescribe drugs, order physical therapy, set fractures, and perform surgery. They also fit corrective inserts called orthotics, design plaster casts and strappings to correct deformities, and design custom-made shoes.

Colleges of podiatric medicine offer a four-year program whose core curriculum is similar to that in other schools of medicine. Graduates receive the degree of Doctor of Podiatric Medicine (DPM). The average earnings ranges from about $60,000 to more than $150,000 per year.

CHIROPRACTOR

Chiropractors are *doctors of chiropractic* or *chiropractic physicians* who diagnose and treat patients whose health problems are associated with the body's muscular, nervous, and skeletal systems, especially the spine. Chiropractors believe that interference with these systems impairs the body's normal functions and lowers its resistance to disease. They also hold that spinal or vertebral dysfunction alters many important body functions by affecting the nervous system and that skeletal imbalance through joint or articular dysfunction, especially in the spine, can cause pain. The chiropractic approach to healthcare is holistic, stressing the patient's overall health and wellness. It recognizes that many factors affect health, including exercise, diet, rest, environment, and heredity. Chiropractors provide natural, drugless, nonsurgical health treatments and rely on the body's inherent recuperative abilities. They also recommend changes in lifestyle—in eating, exercise, and sleeping habits, for example—to their patients. When appropriate, chiropractors consult with and refer patients to other health practitioners. Colleges of chiropractic offer a four-year program whose core curriculum is similar to that in other schools of medicine. Graduates receive the degree of Doctor of Chiropractic. The average earnings ranges from about $50,000 to $120,000 per year.

AUDIOLOGIST

Audiologists work with people who have hearing, balance, and related ear problems. They examine individuals of all ages and identify those with the symptoms of hearing loss and other auditory, balance, and related neural problems. They then assess the nature and extent of the problems and help the individuals manage them. Using audiometers, computers, and other testing devices, they measure the loudness at which a person begins to hear sounds, the ability to distinguish between sounds, and the impact of hearing loss or balance problems on an individual's daily life. Audiologists interpret these results and might coordinate them with medical, educational, and psychological information to make a diagnosis and determine a course of treatment. Audiologists must earn a master's or doctoral degree in audiology from a regionally accredited college or university, achieve a passing score on a national examination in audiology, and demonstrate they have completed a minimum of 2,000 hours of mentored professional practice in a two-year period with a qualified audiologist. Beginning in the year 2007, all applicants must earn a doctoral degree in audiology. Salaries for audiologists range from about $40,000 to $80,000.

BIOMEDICAL ENGINEER

By combining biology and medicine with engineering, biomedical engineers develop devices and procedures that solve medical and health-related problems. Many do research, along with life scientists, chemists, and medical scientists, to develop and evaluate systems and products for use in the fields of biology and health, such as artificial organs, prostheses (artificial devices that replace missing body parts), instrumentation, medical information systems, and health management and care delivery systems. Biomedical engineers design devices used in various medical procedures, such as the computers used to analyze blood or the laser systems used in corrective eye surgery. They develop artificial organs, imaging systems such as magnetic resonance, ultrasound, and x-ray, and devices for automating insulin injections or controlling body functions. A graduate degree is recommended or required for many entry-level jobs. Salaries range from about $50,000 to more than $100,000.

PHARMACIST

Pharmacists dispense drugs prescribed by physicians and other health practitioners and provide information to patients about medications and their use. They advise physicians and other health practitioners on the selection, dosages, interactions, and side effects of medications. Pharmacists also monitor the health and progress of patients in response to drug therapy to ensure safe and effective use of medication. Pharmacists must understand the use, clinical effects, and composition of drugs, including their chemical, biological, and physical properties. Compounding—the actual mixing of ingredients to form powders, tablets, capsules, ointments, and solutions—is a small part of a pharmacist's practice, because most medicines are produced by pharmaceutical companies in a standard dosage and drug delivery form. Traditionally, most pharmacists work in a community setting, such as a retail drugstore, or in a healthcare facility, such as a hospital, nursing home, mental health institution, or neighborhood health clinic. Pharmacy programs grant the degree of Doctor of Pharmacy (Pharm.D.), which requires at least 6 years of postsecondary study and the passing of the licensure examination of a state board of pharmacy. Earnings range from about $55,000 to $100,000.

Wrap Up

In this chapter we looked at many jobs that you can do with a degree in biology. For some of the jobs, advanced degrees are required while for others only a bachelor's degree is necessary. For some jobs you can start with just your bachelor's and take graduate courses toward your master's or doctorate while working. Your salary will reflect both your previous experience and your level of education.

In the next chapter, I will help you to look beyond the want ads and online job search engines to find the job you want using the skills and knowledge you obtained in college or from previous experience.

Chapter 5

Breaking into the Job Market

In the past, college graduates took a job, stayed with the same employer for 25 years or more, and retired with their gold watches and pensions. Well, times have changed. Now, according to the Bureau of Labor Statistics, chances are you'll have at least *nine* different jobs between college and retirement. And that figure might even be low. It's possible you'll change jobs (and even careers) many more times than that, as many as 20 times. Needless to say, learning to find a good job is more than just a sideline. It could be one of the most important things you learn.

In this chapter, we will focus on the job market, helping you to look beyond the want ads and online job search engines to find a job using the skills and knowledge you obtained in college or from previous experience.

These suggestions are geared to current college students, those who have already graduated and are looking for a new job (or career) and those already working in the biological sciences who might want to consider a job change. If you are a high school student looking to find a challenging summer or part-time job, you can use the same basic ideas, recognizing that you may not have the same skill levels or experience.

Planning Ahead

The things that can help you get a job after you graduate are, to start, participating in activities, working with a mentor, volunteering, investigating careers of interest *before* your last semester in college or graduate school, and participating in at least one internship. Students that have followed these guidelines are prepared and have a plan.

If you did not take advantage of these opportunities, you won't be on the same level as those with actual experience in biology-related fields. One thing to keep in mind, however, is that employers and recruiters aren't looking for job hires based on major. Instead, they are looking at skills and characteristics. According to the National Association of Colleges and Employers, the top 10 characteristics that employers look for in prospective hires include (in order of importance):

1. Communication skill

2. Honesty/integrity

3. Teamwork skills

4. Interpersonal skills

5. Motivation/initiative

6. Strong work ethic

7. Analytical skills

8. Flexibility/adaptability

9. Computer skills (basic knowledge of common office applications)

10. Self-confidence

That means if you have made the most of your college career, be sure to stress these qualities in addition to your biology-related experiences, skills, and knowledge. If you didn't quite make the most of your opportunities during college, look for ways you did illustrate the preceding qualities. For example, if you were a cheerleader, you can use this experience to show how you work well with a team as well as highlight your motivation skills. If you were president of your fraternity, you can use your experiences as a communicator, leader, planner, and so on to show how that experience illustrated your mastery of these characteristics.

Searching for a Job

When you're searching for a job, the sheer volume of information you'll need to juggle can quickly become overwhelming. Names, phone numbers, dates and times for appointments, lists of companies and job openings, and all kinds of other details are coming at you. And although everyone makes mistakes sometimes, you certainly don't want to make one that will cost you a job offer. Clearly, getting organized is a major priority. Here are some tips to get you started.

THE BASICS

Experts suggest four basic goals to help you organize yourself for your job search. They are:

- ◆ Effective time management
- ◆ Thorough note-taking
- ◆ An uncluttered work area
- ◆ A workable system of organization

HOW TO BUDGET YOUR TIME

A more specific suggestion from the experts is to spend at least two hours a day working on your job hunt, and to do so six days a week, giving yourself a much-deserved day of rest. Of course, your ability to follow this advice might depend on the schedule you have now, which probably includes classes if you're still in college. However, keep in mind that this is just a suggestion, and you can adapt it to your current situation in whatever way works best for you.

Unfortunately, it's impossible to predict how long your job hunt will take. Beyond the question of how much time you can spend on it each day or week, it will depend on the availability of jobs in the biological sciences, your personal qualifications, the geographic area in which you want to work and live, and any number of random conditions. Experts estimate that searching for a job can take 3 to 12 months, but there's no guarantee. Although there are a lot of aspects of the process you can't control, figuring out how to budget your time is one thing you can do to avoid completely losing control.

Try to calculate how long it takes for you to complete the various tasks involved in your job search. Imagine, for instance, that you need a half hour to an hour to write an individualized cover letter for each résumé you send out, and you want to send out 10 résumés a week, each with its own cover letter. This means you will need to spend between 5 and 10 hours a week writing cover letters. But letter-writing is only one of the steps involved in your job search. You'll need time to gather information about the companies you're applying to and time to follow up on earlier communications. Then you'll need to ensure yourself against time lost to unexpected mishaps, from computer problems to head colds. For this purpose, experts suggest raising the total number of hours you've come up with by 15 percent.

Will you be able to do this? To find the right job, you should assume this kind of commitment will be required.

Your next step is to look at your pre-existing schedule and see whether you can fit in these new job-hunting chores. You might find that you need to take time from some of your other activities, at least temporarily.

YOUR JOB SEARCH BOOK

A job search book is a great organizational tool that you can create for yourself. You can keep all your information in one place, carry it with you to your college's career office, and store it easily on your desk or bookshelf. Since it will be portable, it would be easier than storing everything on your computer. If you're comfortable using a PDA, that will be effective but won't allow you to store the paperwork you receive from companies.

To make a job search book, get a three-ring binder with pocket dividers and use it to keep track of all the information and paperwork that you acquire in the process. File cover letters and responses, write notes about potential employers, and keep a communication log for all kinds of correspondence, from telephone conversations to postal to email, including reminders to follow up on previous communication. Include calendar pages to keep track of appointments and directory pages to keep track of your contacts, cross-referencing the information in your communications log. You should also keep spare copies of your résumé in one of the pockets, along with copies of any research papers and articles you've written, which some employers might ask to see. Use other pockets for postage stamps and other supplies, as well as business cards, ads, and brochures you may pick up along the way.

You might organize all of this information in a variety of ways, and even reorganize it as your search progresses. At first, you might organize job opportunities by salary, location, or other characteristics that are important to you. This may help you decide on which opportunities to focus your attention.

Later, when a first contact begins to yield results, you can move your copy of the initial cover letter to its own section of the binder, where it can be followed up with further communication, records of interviews, and other information. Jot down basic information about the potential employer, perhaps on the section divider. This includes the company address, phone number, and Web site, along with the names of relevant people at the company, such as your interviewer and the interviewer's personal assistant.

DON'T BELIEVE THE CLICHÉS

A lot of words of wisdom about job hunting are passed around, but they tend to be rather absolute, encouraging you to accept or reject entire strategies, from networking to want ads to agencies to cold-calling. The only cliché that might actually have some truth to it is that you shouldn't put all your eggs in one basket. If you can put several of these strategies to work for you, you'll significantly increase your chances of success.

If you're planning to devote an hour or two each day to your job hunt, it might make sense to focus on a different strategy as you go through your week, a rotation schedule that will help you stay organized while allowing time for mail to be delivered, letters to be read, and so forth. You might begin the week with the newspaper's help wanted section, circling the advertisements on paper copies you want to reply to and sending online job postings to yourself and storing them in a separate folder. Then during that day, you can respond to the announcements.

The next day, you might contact an employment agency or professional organization that accommodates recent graduates with biology degrees. The day after that you could devote your time to networking with people who are in a position to help you find a job, from professors to internship supervisors you've worked with, to friends and relatives who happen to be in relevant professions. Use another day to stop by your college's office for job placement and career planning, where you can check the latest postings and look up alumni who have offered to advise people entering their field. When your networking day comes around again, you can get in touch with these alumni.

Yet another day can be used for an Internet job search and to research potential employers online in order to educate yourself about a company you might want to join. Finally, you might want to use your final day's time to prepare a mass mailing of "cold" letters to some of these companies, even if they have not advertised any openings. Of course, you should leave time each day to return any calls or emails that come in as a result of your search so that you don't keep anyone waiting.

This proposed schedule is merely a suggestion, of course, and you might find a different arrangement that works better for you. Furthermore, there will be days when you'll have to deviate from this schedule to accommodate holidays, exams, part-time jobs, classes, and other obligations. The point is to plan some sort of job-hunting routine that will help you stay on-task and organized.

STAY INFORMED AND BE REALISTIC

Learning about the business of your desired career is crucial to finding that first job for three main reasons:

◆ You'll be better able to decide whether this is a good situation for you, given the hours, location, size of the company, salary, and other factors beyond your knowledge of biology.

◆ You'll impress potential employers for having done your homework and learned about their company, whether you're sending out unsolicited résumés with individually tailored cover letters, or whether you're actually being interviewed for a position.

◆ You'll be able to make realistic decisions about the best way to look for a job, given the current climate in this field.

Another way of being realistic is to consider your own strengths, both inner and outer. One of the case studies later in the book is a woman who did a lot of cold calling and got a great job. It worked for her because her personality is well-suited to cold calls. But despite her success, this method doesn't work as well for someone who is very shy or introverted or who tends to stutter when nervous. You might have similar issues with other job-hunting strategies, and although you probably can't avoid those strategies altogether, you would be better off focusing more on the ones that are better suited to your inclinations.

By outer strengths, I mean any special resources or contacts you can use. You might have a cousin who works in a pharmaceutical company that needs staff, or a roommate who volunteers at the local zoo and can introduce you to the person in charge. The graduate student who was a teaching assistant in one of your biology classes might be going into a specialty that interests you as well. Even if some of these people don't have jobs to offer—they might not actually be employers themselves— they can certainly give you advice or introduce you to the right people. This also increases the chances that when you do meet with a potential employer, you will be more than just another applicant. You'll stand out as someone personally recommended by a mutual acquaintance.

Take Advantage of Current Trends

Times change, the economy changes, the job market changes, and the conditions that prevailed when your parents were graduating college might have changed beyond recognition. That said, here are some things to consider in your own search for a job.

◆ *Companies downsize.*

On one hand, this might imply that the company isn't hiring new workers and that it wouldn't be realistic to apply. On the other hand, although downsizing means that existing employees will lose their jobs, it also might mean that someone has to pick up the slack, especially during the transition period. For example, an agency that has a team of five professional researchers might find itself facing budget cuts. The agency might deal with these budget cuts by replacing four of the professional, high-paid staff with two or three unlicensed recent graduates who can work under the supervision of the remaining researchers. Newly hired staff, particularly those straight out of college, can be paid less while helping the agency or lab manage its remaining work.

◆ *Underemployment has its perks.*

By now, you might be considering several different careers based on your biology degree, but you're not sure which one to pursue. You might be able to try one out by taking a job for which you are overqualified. This will give you a chance to explore the roles played by other employees, as well as leaving you with enough energy after work to take a class, do a part-time internship, or whatever else will help you make your decision. You won't want to be underemployed forever, but it can be a useful source of at least some income and experience, especially when the job market is bad. You might decide to keep the job only until you finish your coursework, or for a year, or until whatever time limit makes sense to you.

◆ *Your interests might fit into a new field.*

As technology has continued to enter new fields, new roles have developed for people with degrees in biology. A prime example is the increasing role of genetics and stem-cell research. Although these may not be areas you studied extensively, you might find you have an interest in them and could do some "learning on the job."

Similarly, you might find that in addition to the technical aspects of biology, you also love marketing and/or sales. Pharmaceutical companies are almost always looking for recent graduates with degrees in biology to fit into their sales and marketing teams. This might not have been an area you learned in college, but the company can teach you the nontechnical skills while you bring to this kind of job your knowledge of biology.

◆ *The workplace has changed.*

As you already know, people with degrees in biology can be found working in a wide variety of settings. Ironically, those working in medicine or sales in successful companies usually make the most money. But it takes time and experience to build up such a medical practice or develop a client base, so it might not be the first thing to try right out of school.

Contingency employment, which includes temporary, part-time, and contract work, saves employers the cost of a full-time employee, because they don't have to pay for healthcare and other benefits, or keep paying extra workers during the slow season. Laboratories might bring in recent college graduates for a while to work with the full-time staff when new contracts are won. For you, there are two advantages to this kind of employment: it's increasingly available when the job market is poor, and it allows you the time to pursue a graduate degree, raise children, or tend to other matters in your life. The down side is that the pay is lower; benefits are nonexistent; and, if it's a temporary or contract job, it won't last forever. However, a contingency job can become a full-time, permanent position as funding improves and your contributions are recognized.

How to Network

Many corporate employers participate in on-campus recruitment events for graduating seniors. However, although there are biology positions in the corporate world, most jobs in the field are in noncorporate settings, such as labs and governmental offices, so you might have to go beyond this ready-made networking scenario.

If you're interested in an employer who does not participate in these recruitment events, start at your campus office of career services. There might be business cards or contact information on file, especially if any of your school's recent alumni applied for jobs with that employer. You might be able to contact an actual employee who went to your college or even the recruiter or interviewer who was involved.

Even if there isn't a job to apply for, your new contact might be willing to set up an informational interview to talk about future and possible career goals. If you make a good impression, you might be remembered as a prospective candidate when a job does open up, but be careful not to pressure your contact about this when he or she is giving you the courtesy of chatting with you!

Another wonderful resource is student membership in a professional organization. Most such organizations offer low rates for students and provide networking opportunities as well as information on getting an advanced degree, job postings, and conferences where you can do more networking. See the Appendix at the end of this book for more information on professional organizations.

Social Networks

You already have a network of friends, relatives, and acquaintances who can help you find a job. Consider all the people you know, even casually: Besides family members and professors, there are classmates, roommates, neighbors, and teammates. Both on and off campus, you might belong to a club, a congregation, or a fraternity or sorority. There are people you meet at the gym, people you know from high school or summer camp, or even co-workers from your part-time or work-study job. And all of these people know other people who might be directly involved in a career that involves biology. Your workout buddy from the gym might be majoring in a completely different subject, but it might have come up in conversation that he or she has a parent who works in the specialty that interests you. Given your connection to the family, the parent might be willing—and even flattered—to speak with you. Just remember to show appropriate gratitude. Buy your buddy a drink, write a thank-you note to the parent, or do whatever seems appropriate in the context of your relationship.

Another great tactic is to do volunteer work in a capacity that's related to your field. This is harder to do in one of the sciences, like biology, than it might be in psychology or education, but there are possibilities. For example, you might be able to help out at the local zoo, as one of the women we feature in the next chapter did, or at an animal clinic, allowing you to use your knowledge of anatomy and physiology. Become a tutor for high school kids (or even lower-division college students on campus). You'll not only gain valuable experience, which will look great on a graduate school or job application, but you'll also be able to network with the supervising professionals at these locations.

Maintain Your Network

After you've found all these contacts—although you should never stop adding new ones—keep track of them. Keep the relationship alive in appropriate ways, which might include sending holiday greeting cards, emailing a periodic update about your progress and any address changes, and extending your congratulations on any promotions or other accomplishments. The idea is to remind your contacts that you exist in a pleasant way that makes them care what happens to you, at least professionally. You don't want to pester them with requests for them to reply to you or take up their time, or they might regret ever having met with you. You do want them to remember you as a nice person who will come to mind when they need to recommend someone for a job!

ONLINE JOB SEARCHES

Like other job-hunting techniques, online searches have their advantages and disadvantages. Advantages include

- ◆ Being able to find jobs in distant places, in case you are not planning to stay in your college town or want to consider all appropriate jobs, regardless of location

- ◆ Searching a wide variety of sources in one session, from individual companies to the college career service site to placement sites specializing in careers in science

- ◆ Ease of applying: With a click of a mouse, your résumé and cover letter are submitted. There are no letters to stamp, mail, or get lost in transit.

- ◆ Preinterviewing: Some companies provide an online questionnaire to help narrow down the field of applicants. If they like your answers, they can call you in for a real interview.

Then there are the disadvantages, most notably the fact that you face more competition, as applicants from all over the country—or even the world—vie for the same job.

The tricky part is making your application stand out while still following the guidelines provided by the site. The site might state that you should not send attachments, for example, which would make it hard to include that research article you published last semester. One way around this might be to include a link in your résumé that will take the employer to a site where your article is posted.

Even if the site does not warn about attachments, keep in mind the amount of data you are sending, at least from a technological viewpoint. Some agencies and employers will not permit attachments to go through because of firewalls and will reject your entire email.

You can check out some important Web sites in the Appendix. These sites can help you find both entry-level and professional positions.

What can you gain from your Internet search? While you are hoping to find a job opening perfect for you, don't overlook the other information you can get from this search:

◆ What are the "hottest" jobs? What are the most advertised jobs?

◆ Read the advice at the various sites to see how you can improve your chances of getting a job. (Ignore for the most part companies or advisors that make promises to improve your resume and guarantees success *all* for one low payment of. . . . You shouldn't have to pay for advice, especially on résumés or other common job hunting topics such as interviewing.)

◆ Look for companies or jobs of interest. Although you might not get the job through the site postings, reading through the types of jobs that are available and the companies that are hiring can help you pinpoint the exact position you seek.

Preparing Your Résumé

You can include the following characteristics in your résumé, which you should prepare and have available. You'll need your résumé for career fairs and actual job interviews. You can find entire books on creating a winning résumé. This chapter summarizes some of the key points, especially useful for finding jobs in the psychology or related field.

Consider these suggestions:

◆ Include all your pertinent contact information.

◆ Rather than list your career objective (the job you seek) at the top, begin with a strong selling point, a list of your key skills and experiences. Highlight your key knowledge, experiences, and characteristics. Summarize why someone should hire you. Succinctly include in a short list what you have to offer.

◆ Highlight any biology-related experience, including internships, mentoring, volunteer work, and so on. Don't just list your experience, "Designed Independent Research Study, September 2003 to September 2004." Go beyond the specifics of the title and dates and explain what you did. Show what skills you learned or practiced from this experience, such as "Wrote Methodology Section of published paper and performed statistical data analysis to determine significance."

◆ Be sure to *sell* all your activities, not just those related directly to biology. Think of how you spent your time and whether during your college career there's anything else worth mentioning. For instance, perhaps during the summer you organized and volunteered at a charity golf outing. Or perhaps during elections you worked with a political party or candidate. Don't just focus on the obvious.

◆ Include any and all relevant work experiences in addition to college. Although some jobs may seem to have nothing to offer (perhaps your first job was selling ice cream at the mall), perhaps the fact that you started working at 15 to pay for your private high school education makes mentioning that job worthwhile.

◆ When you think of job tasks, recast them in business terms, which even laboratories relate to. In general, it's a good idea to tie the job experience to the field of biology or science. For instance, suppose that you created a kiddie newsletter as your job as summer camp counselor; you could include the ability to create and publish appropriate, informative types of communication. This information would be useful if you are applying for a job that will require that you write research reports.

◆ Use the resources at your career center to prepare your resume. They not only are likely to have several books and examples in their library, but also should have career counselors that can critique and provide feedback on your resume.

You might also consider having business cards printed up with your name and contact information. These are easy to pass out, especially when networking.

Career Center, On-Campus Recruiters, and Career Fairs

In addition to publications and Web sites, your campus career center might sponsor career fairs or host on-campus recruiters. (You can also find career fairs held through other sources, such as your local paper.) These are yet another possible source of job openings. How to best take advantage of these events? Consider the following advice:

◆ Find out who's going to attend. If the fair, for instance, is geared toward the medical field (a field that seems to always be in need of employees), you might decide to take a close look at the types of workers they seek. If they are basically looking for nurses or anyone in the nursing field, and there aren't any opportunities for biology-related medical careers, you might consider skipping the fair.

◆ If the career fair is not limited to one area, take a look at the various companies that plan to attend. Are there any companies of interest to you? If so, make a list so that when you are at the fair, you can focus on these companies.

◆ Dress for an interview (at least a casual interview). Don't go in sweatpants and a t-shirt even if you think you are just browsing through. If someone wants to do an interview on the spot, you should be dressed for the part (or at least close enough given the casualness of the setting).

◆ Prepare a short statement (some people call this the "elevator speech"). This should sum up your education, experience, and career interest. Memorize it so that you get your main points across, but make sure that when you "recite" it, you do so with enthusiasm while adding pertinent facts and details based on the situation.

◆ If you are asked what type of job you are looking for, be precise in explaining. If they are not hiring in that area, ask whether they might know or recommend someone that is or might be looking for someone with your skills—more networking. Ask them to keep you in mind. Again, this person may hold on to your résumé and pass it along if a colleague mentions he's looking to hire someone.

◆ If you do participate in an interview (or several) be sure to ask how the process works. For instance, if they ask for your résumé, does that mean they plan to call? Or are they just keeping it on file? If you do an initial interview, what's the next step? How should you follow up? What should you expect to hear from them? Don't walk away without knowing what is supposed to happen next.

Find Your Own Job Openings

Often you identify in your career search a particular company or organization for which you want to work. You can approach them directly to inquire about jobs. You can check their Web page for openings or talk to human resources about current and upcoming positions.

Sometimes you'll take an entry-level position at a company just to get started. After you're hired, you'll gain the advantage of getting experience at that actual company. And because many jobs aren't advertised but are filled from within, you are now one of the insiders. Once inside, you can keep alert to any possible new job positions and be first in line for consideration (sometimes even before the job has formally been posted).

Sometimes the job you want hasn't been created. Although you might have a hard time getting someone to listen to you and to sell this job to, it can be done. This strategy works best if you are already working for your ideal company. You then can spot the need for this job, create your job based on this need and your desires, and then "sell" the position to the company. You'll have more success if you show them how the new job solves a problem, improves a situation, adds revenue, or provides some tangible benefit for the company.

In trying to create your own job, look for economic, business, and demographic trends. For instance, the Baby Boomers are nearing retirement. Around 77 million Americans will start hitting retirement age in 2010. What does that mean for you as someone with a background in biology? What markets, jobs, and needs might these people have for someone with your skills? This population will need more drugs to combat diseases, will need more medical attention, help with insurance programs, activity programs for retired seniors, and so on. Take all these needs and consider what need you can fulfill by creating a specific job or by looking for an existing job in this market (which is likely to expand). Look for other demographic or economic trends and the opportunities they may present.

Interviewing for a Job

When you are asked for an interview, don't expect to put on your newly shined shoes and be ready. You have some work to do. First, you need to research the company and organization. Second, you need to practice for the interview, anticipating the types of questions you'll be asked and preparing great responses. Third, you need to know how to follow up after the interview. This section discusses these skills.

Do Your Research

Before the interview, you should research the organization to find out more about them (What products do they make? What services do they offer? Who's the president or head of the company/organization? Is it a public or private company? How many people are employed there? Are there multiple locations? Where is the headquarters?). You should know the answers to these and other key questions about the company or organization.

Where can you find the information? To start, visit the company or organization's Web site. Most companies include a page "about us" or something similar. They might talk about the company history, the mission statement, and so on. Look also for pages that describe how the company is organized as well as who holds key positions. (Note these names.)

In addition, search the Internet for news stories about the company. Have they been in the news recently? If so, why? Are they launching a new product? Cutting back? Have they won any awards? Try to make sure you are up-to-date on any current news relating to the company.

You might also consider visiting sites that provide company overviews, such as Hoovers.com or Vault.com. These sites include profiles of thousands of companies and include more detailed research about the specific company. For the most part, you can look up general information about the company at these sites. For complete, detailed information, you might need to be a subscriber (pay a fee). Check with your school; they might have accounts with these types of sites. You might be able to get the detailed information going through your school's career center's connection.

As another source, if you know someone that works or has worked for that company, you might want to talk to that person. He or she might give you a better sense of the company atmosphere as well as what they look for in potential employees.

PRACTICE

In addition to doing your research, you should also prepare for the interview. In general, plan for five key points you want to make in the interview. Keep this in mind: These are what you want the interviewer to remember about you. Also, be prepared to answer these typical questions:

◆ What do you know about our . . . (company, organization, and so on.)? (Here's where that research pays off!)

◆ Tell me about yourself.

◆ What are your strengths/weaknesses?

◆ What would you like to change about yourself?

◆ Why did you leave your last job?

◆ Where do you see yourself five years from now?

◆ What are your goals?

◆ Why should I hire you?

In general, focus on what you can do for the company. Tell the interviewer what makes you unique as a person, what special skills you have, and what distinguishes you from the other people who want this same job. Stress the preparation work you have done and the experiences and skills you already have for this position.

INTERVIEW TIPS

In addition to being prepared for the questions, keep in mind the following tips:

◆ Dress appropriately. If you've visited the company perhaps on an information interview, you should get a sense of how they dress. Know the night before what you're going to wear and make sure it's ready—no trying to find those nylons without a run in them or pants that aren't missing a button at the last minute.

◆ Be on time. No excuses.

◆ Use a firm handshake and be sure to remember the person's name. (Say it again after you meet; this should help you remember.) If they have a card, you might ask for one. You can also provide your résumé (and business card, if you have one).

◆ When you ask a question, be precise and to the point. Don't blab on and on. Emphasize your strengths and show how your experience or education make you a good fit for the position.

◆ Stick to professional issues. Other topics such as a mutual acquaintance or an upcoming event might pop up. Remember this is an interview, not a conversation with a potential buddy.

THE INTERVIEW AND FOLLOW UP

At the end of the interview, the interviewer will usually ask whether you have any questions. You should have some questions prepared, but don't just ask a question because you're supposed to do so and have already prepared one. It's possible your question will have been already answered in the interview. Above all else, don't ask "Well, do I get the job?" (Also, don't ask about salary, vacation, or benefits in the first interview. Save these questions for later interviews when you are negotiating for the position.)

Instead, ask questions to learn more about the employer and company. For instance, you might ask how that person got his or her start. Ask for additional information about the position, what skills are needed, and what resources are available. Also, try to get a sense of where the company is in the job hiring process. Do they have more people to interview? How soon will they be making an offer? When do they anticipate the person to start his or her employment?

It's key that you know how the overall interview process works. In many organizations, particularly as you get to higher up positions, there are initial interviews and follow-up interviews. You'll want to know what to expect and how many times you'll need to come back before a hiring decision is made. Some of that might depend on your strength and the strength of the applicant pool. But by inquiring about the process, you'll at least have the framework for how the decision will be made.

Also make sure that you know what to do next. Should you call the person who interviewed you? Will he or she call you? If so, by what date? If you haven't been called by that date, you will need to know whether it's okay if you call. Interviewing takes patience, but there's no sense waiting for a call if it's not going to come. So it's perfectly reasonable to ask whether you can call after a certain time limit to check on the job progress.

Be sure you send a thank-you note immediately after the interview. Hand-written notes are best—little touches such as this make a difference. You might find hand-written notes antiquated in the age of email, but doing things "right" can make a big impression. Don't just say thank you in the note, but restate your interest in the job as well as some of the reasons you think you are the perfect match for the position. (Even if you don't want the job after the interview, still send a thank-you note, but skip the parts about how you are a perfect match.)

If possible, find out what happens if you didn't get the job. Whom did they hire? Was the position dropped? Did they hire from within? Use this information to evaluate your interview skills. Did someone more qualified get the position? There's not too much you can do about that except look for opportunities to increase your experience. Did someone you consider equal to you get the job (a fellow student, for example)? Perhaps he or she did a better job in the interview. What might you do better next time? Use each experience to better prepare you for your next chance. Also, be sure to ask the potential employer to pass along your résumé to other's looking to fill similar positions.

Wrap Up

In this chapter I reviewed strategies for securing a good job in the biology field. I discussed how important it is to be organized and to budget your time on the job search activities, how to take advantage of opportunities that come along, and how to maximize your chances by networking. I also gave some pointers on sprucing up your résumé and interviewing techniques.

In the next chapter, I will introduce you to six people who were biology majors in college and went on to interesting jobs. I'll describe what they do and why they majored in biology. I'll tell you how they think their undergraduate degree in bio prepared them for their current jobs, what other training they got, and what particularly helpful moves they made to get where they are now. I describe what they love about their jobs and also what they could do without. And I'll give you some of my own thoughts about their careers.

Chapter 6

Case Studies

In this section, you will meet six young professionals who majored in biological science in college. But as you will see, they have each gone on to very different careers, some directly related to their degrees, some less so.

Karen, Epidemiologist

In this first case study, you are introduced to Karen, an epidemiologist. As you read about Karen, please note some of the keys to her success that you might be in a position to emulate:

♦ She explored within her major by taking an undergraduate epidemiology course.

♦ She created her own internship within this specialty.

♦ She paid attention to a guest lecturer, enabling him to motivate and inspire her career choice.

♦ She did the research to know that her career choice would require graduate school coursework.

♦ In graduate school, she worked part-time for the state health department, gaining valuable experience.

WHAT I DO

I work at a federal health agency as an epidemiologist where we study the causes, distribution, and control of diseases. I am currently working on a research project in which we are studying patients who have gotten discharged from hospitals. We're looking at their diagnoses, the procedures they underwent, and the outcomes and comparing that across demographic criteria, socioeconomic criteria, and really, just about every other variable we can to see whether we can determine any significant differences. As part of this small research group, I'm involved with lot of areas, including operations, analysis, and writing reports. Although I've done some complex statistical analysis in the past, at the agency we have others who do this full time and are true experts. Of course, my team works with those people. This is just one of the studies I've worked on since becoming an epidemiologist; some of the others dealt with immunizations and vaccinations. I also have worked in a public health office.

WHY I MAJORED IN BIOLOGY

I always liked biology, especially in high school. I specifically liked learning about animals, humans, and the life sciences. I wasn't grossed out by blood, but I never really wanted to be a doctor like so many of the other bio majors—it just wasn't right for me. For one thing I didn't want to work 80 billion hours, which you often have to do as a doctor. I wanted a life. Lifestyle is important to me. While I liked biology, I didn't know what I would do with a degree in it. Fortunately, in my college we didn't have to specialize in one area so I was able to take lots of courses in different areas of bio, like microbiology, zoology, anatomy, and physiology. I don't think that's possible in many schools, and in fact, even where I went they don't offer a general biology major any more. It wasn't until my junior year that I actually took a course in epidemiology. A friend of mine had taken it and recommended that I do also. But before I signed up for the course I did some of my own research to see if that was what I wanted to take. I read about disease outbreaks and decided to take the course. That turned out to be a great decision for me.

How the Biology Major Prepared Me for My Job

I never really thought about how being a bio major has helped me as an epidemiologist, but I guess it has helped me a lot. In college, I took anatomy and physiology courses which, at the time, I thought would be a waste since I wasn't going to go to medical school. It turns out that that knowledge has really helped. In fact, a lot of epidemiologists have actually attended medical school and are MDs, so the biology I took in college—the anatomy and physiology especially—helps me converse with them and understand a lot more than if I didn't have that background. In fact, with the study I am working on now that anatomy and physiology really comes in handy since we have to know a lot about the human body to understand the diagnoses and procedures. Also, since we do a lot of research and are always writing and reading technical reports, we have to be familiar with scientific method and technical journals. As a bio major, we had to read many technical articles, learn statistical analysis, and understand experimental design, which is directly related to what I do now.

Other Training

When I was taking the one and only undergraduate epidemiology course offered in college, we had a guest lecturer, an expert on the spread of mad cow disease. In fact, he was *the* non-British expert. He was the government official appearing on the Oprah show when she announced that she wouldn't eat beef any more because of the fear of mad cow. His lecture was so inspirational to me, so I wanted to take more epidemiology classes. Unfortunately, the undergraduate division in my college didn't offer any other courses. So I looked around at the different graduate programs to see whether there were other courses. I talked to the professor who had given the lecture—he was actually working in the vet school—and he told me that although they did offer another epi course in the vet school, and I would be welcome to take it, it wouldn't be offered again until the fall. Here it was spring of my junior year so I would have to wait. But then he suggested that I work with him in a sort of independent study/internship for that semester and take the other epi course later on. That turned out to be one of the most important things I ever did for my career. I learned so much and was able to work with the very best, as I said, *the* non-British expert on mad cow disease. About that time, I realized that if I wanted to get anywhere in the field, I would have to go to graduate school. So I applied to various schools and chose the one where I could get my Masters in Public Health (MPH) with a specialty in epidemiology. After that I decided to continue my education and went on to a Ph.D. program.

HELPFUL MOVES

Creating my own specialty by doing the internship with the professor in the veterinary school was definitely the best thing I ever did and was really a great break. I have to take credit for creating that opportunity for myself. But I admit I was lucky that he was there and was able to offer me the chance to work with him. I also got very lucky in graduate school, although it was a result of a national tragedy. I was in graduate school working on my master's and doing part time work in the state health department when 9/11 happened. Right after the attack, you'll remember, people were really afraid of bioterrorism. That was also the time when we had those anthrax scares. As an expert, even though I was a graduate student, I got to be one of the people working on the response team. I was answering phone calls and dealing with the concerns people had. I became the point of contact, the liaison between the state health agency and the state laboratory that did all the tests on infections. Also at the same time, the West Nile Virus began hitting where I was and that meant the health department also had to deal with that crisis. All of this gave me so much experience and insight into what a career in epidemiology would be like, although sadly it was because of such an awful time for the country.

Another thing that helped me was when I was in graduate school working on an HIV study. We were looking at adherence to medication and substance abuse in HIV patients. I did data collection, data entry, and even helped write the manuscript. Even though we didn't have any findings to report, the paper actually did get presented. The paper essentially said that we *didn't* find what we were looking for. That opened my eyes, and I've learned that what happened to us is not unusual. It's a shame, really, that so much money is spent on studies that produce no findings and that rarely get reported. I mean about the "no finding," not that money was spent. It's appropriate spending because we learn a lot with a "no finding." I wish more people would realize that.

PITFALLS TO AVOID

There are a couple of things I can say here. First is about attending graduate school. To go anywhere in the field of epidemiology, you absolutely have to have a graduate degree. But when you're first starting out in college, you may not necessarily know right away that that's what you want. So, instead of jumping into a particular field, which may or may not be right for you, get a good background in statistics, health sciences, public health, sociology, anatomy, and physiology—lots of different areas of biology.

The second thing I want to say is that you shouldn't let barriers stop you. If you run into an obstacle, look around for other opportunities, like I did when my school didn't offer any more undergraduate courses in epidemiology. Think "outside of the box." In most schools, you can do an independent study directly for a specific professor. And in some, you can actually create your own major.

WHAT I LOVE ABOUT MY JOB

I truly love the flexibility of the work itself! I can work on different aspects in epidemiology, different projects, and use the same skills I learned. Plus, there are lots of different options for me in this same field: surveys, immunizations, public health, a lot of things. But I guess the best thing about my job is what I do. It's helpful. It's doing good things. As an epidemiologist, I can have a direct impact on peoples' lives. Many of my colleagues have that same feeling.

THINGS ON THE JOB I COULD DO WITHOUT

I can definitely do without people thinking that epidemiology is the study of skin! I get that a lot.

Seriously, one thing that comes to mind here is that I'm not a big fan of government red tape. I know we have to deal with it, but that's not the part of the job I love. And another thing I can do without is the lack of funding in this country for public health issues. Here in my current job we don't have a problem because we're federally funded and are okay. But in other places, and especially in academia where many of my colleagues work, there's a lot of pressure to bring in funds. Plus there's that whole public or perish mentality.

My Work and My Life

This particular job in epidemiology has regular 9-to-5 hours, something that I really like. When I was working at a county health office during and right after September 11, things were very crazy. But here, it's fairly steady work. Of course, there are some times when we have to work late to get something done. But not too often. And epidemiologist pay is pretty good, and I get to work with very smart people. I'm always learning a lot, and I love the fact that what I do can really help people.

I was really lucky to have gotten into epidemiology when I did, that is, pre-9/11. As a result of this national tragedy, there is a lot more focus on what we do and, as a result, we have a lot more opportunities. After all, when the President goes on national TV and mentions your field, you know you're pretty safe in your job. And you're doing work that matters.

Salaries for Epidemiologists

As a general rule, epidemiologists straight out of school (usually with a graduate degree) earn from about $45,000 to $80,000, with most starting in the $50,000 range.

Some Thoughts About Karen's Career

Karen loved biology but because she wasn't interested in becoming a doctor, she didn't know what she could do with a major in bio. When she found something about which she was excited, she used her initiative to continue taking courses in the field. And as so often happens when you are enthusiastic about something, opportunities open themselves to you. In Karen's case, she took advantage of the professor's offer to do an independent study with him. But her strong background in many areas of biology have helped her, not only in her job, but also in the fact that she found a career she loves.

Susan: Education and Outreach Program Manager

In this case study, you are introduced to Susan, an education and outreach program manager. As you read about Susan, please note some of the keys to her success that you might be in a position to emulate:

◆ She explored her options after graduation by taking an internship and similar positions.

◆ She developed a love of teaching and wasn't afraid to go back to school to get her master's degree and teaching certificate.

◆ Not satisfied with teaching middle school, she searched for other options and found an education and outreach position.

What I Do

I do a lot of different things in this job. My title is Education and Outreach Program Manager at a professional society of biologists. But that doesn't begin to explain what I actually do. First, I work with a committee of college biology teachers who look at the biology curriculum for undergraduates. As part of that responsibility we did a survey where we looked at the National Academy's recommendations to see which were implemented and how well they worked. I also write a column for the members of the association in which I discuss things such as different college programs, teaching strategies, and the use of computers in the curriculum. I get to use my writing skills a lot. I'm also coordinating a symposium for a national association of biology teachers, and this requires incredible attention to detail. I've been involved in just about every aspect of running this conference, from room assignments to developing the program, getting panelists, working with the hotel, you name it. And lastly, because I work so closely with the members, there are always these *ad hoc* tasks I have to take on because the committees and members always have lots of ideas and initiatives.

WHY I MAJORED IN BIOLOGY

My mother is a doctor—a pathologist—and my father is an electrical engineer. They were both my role models. So early on, I was really gung ho about biomedical engineering, the combination of the two disciplines. In fact, when I first started out in college I started in electrical engineering. But later on I switched over to biology. I guess I never really considered anything else because I liked it so much.

HOW THE BIOLOGY MAJOR PREPARED ME FOR MY JOB

Even with all the biology I took in college, and the work I've done since, I don't remember most of the facts (I had to relearn a lot when I was teaching middle school bio). But I developed a strong foundation in biology and that has helped me form common grounds with the biologists and educators I work with. We speak the same language and since communication with the members of our association is one of the most important parts of my job, my background has been a significant help.

OTHER TRAINING

When I got to be a senior in college, I really had no idea what I wanted to do after graduation. I knew I wanted to do something in biology, but I had no idea what. I had taken different bio courses and liked almost all of them, from aquaculture to zoology, but I wasn't sure what to do. So I spent an entire summer scouring the books looking for an internship—in anything and anywhere. I applied for a million positions and finally, finally, while I was away on a trip, I got a call from my mother saying someone wanted me to work in an environmental education center on the South Carolina coast. I jumped at it. What a terrific job. I made all of $125 per week, plus room and board, and I worked really hard teaching school groups about beach ecology and maritime forests. After that internship, I went on to something very similar in the Florida keys at an outdoor science center. This time, we got to go out on boats so the curriculum was more than just beach ecology. Then I went to the Smoky Mountains in North Carolina where I got to do the same kind of thing.

Finally I realized that I loved teaching so I went back to school to get my master's degree and teaching certificate. After I finished, I taught middle school science for three years. I was totally overwhelmed with the demands of the work, so I started looking around for some other kinds of options. I did an exhaustive Web search and found a job doing education and outreach—not where I am now but at another society. I never even knew there was such a thing as education outreach.

HELPFUL MOVES

I think there were three distinct moves I made that were particularly helpful in getting me where I am. The first was when I went through all those books and applied for all those internships. It was hard work completing all the applications, but it really paid off.

The second move was when I went to South Carolina to work at the environmental education center. The people in the program trained me and I learned so much that way because I had to immediately teach what I had learned. It also made me realize how much I liked teaching, or rather, being part of the education community.

And finally, the third move that was significant was my Web search when I found my first job as an education and outreach coordinator.

PITFALLS TO AVOID

In any job, in any field, you're going to have to do more than just what you were trained for. In my case, for example, I have to do a lot of public speaking and writing. Too often students focus on just their discipline and I don't think that's the best way to succeed. I think it's important to not get too specialized and to take a broad curriculum. I think students also need to develop their communication skills by taking public speaking and writing classes.

WHAT I LOVE ABOUT MY JOB

I absolutely love working with the faculty members who are really into what students understand. It's inspiring to work with people who are passionate about what they do, and it's even better that I get to help them do their jobs better. I also love coordinating things, keeping track of lots of details. Running the symposium is all about attention to detail. And I also love writing. There's a solid feeling you get when you get to complete your article and have it published.

THINGS ON THE JOB I COULD DO WITHOUT

A lot of the time I don't have face-to-face contact with the people I work with. Partly that's because I often work out of my home. But even when I'm in the office, the members are not there. The committee members are spread around the country so often I'm working with these people either through email or telephone. I'd much prefer the personal contact.

MY WORK AND MY LIFE

For the most part, my job is essentially a 9-to-5 job. Yes, I work some longer hours when it's needed. But that's not too often. When I was teaching, I was constantly working. I had no weekends, no evenings. I'm sure part of that was because I was new. But I think good teachers work very long hours and take work home with them all the time. This job is not like that. It's hard work, but I'm not totally stressed out about it. And the weekends are mine for me to spend with my family. Also, I have a wonderful feeling when I'm working. I know I'm doing good work and for a great cause. The people I work with and for—the members—are so committed to their work, and that helps motivate me. But I also love the freedom I have to do so many different things, like writing and public speaking. I get to go to a few conferences and meetings every year in some nice places, which I like. And I get to speak to small and large groups, something else I enjoy.

SALARIES FOR EPIDEMIOLOGISTS

Biology teachers don't make a great deal of money, particularly straight out of school. Susan taught for many years and her current job is built around the fact that she had that background. Starting teachers earn only about $30,000 to $35,000, depending on where you teach and the grade-level. Those with advanced degrees earn higher amounts, and experience teachers earn $60,000 and above for the nine-month year.

SOME THOUGHTS ABOUT SUSAN'S CAREER

Susan knew she loved biology but even as she approached college graduation did not know what she would do. She used her initiative to scour the internship opportunities and stumbled upon something she fell in love with, namely, teaching. Doing an internship can be a wonderful way to learn more about a field through experience.

Sara, Zookeeper/Biologist in the Birdhouse

In this case study, you are introduced to Sara, a biologist who does zookeeping work. As you read about Sara, please note some of the keys to her success that you might be in a position to emulate:

◆ She explored her interest in animals early, in high school, and actually was able to eliminate one potential field of study before going to college.

◆ She took a variety of courses within her specialty to prepare for working with different animals in captivity.

◆ She volunteered at a zoo and applied for positions as they opened up.

◆ She accepted a position that she didn't really want, but that was at the zoo where she wanted to work, and has come to love the job!

WHAT I DO

My official title is Biologist, but more than half of my job is keeper at the birdhouse. There are two biologists and eight keepers, but, as I said, two-thirds of the time I do keeper work. That means feeding, cleaning, and observation. But the rest of my job is research in my specialty, helping the vets as needed, training the birds, and keeping track of all the outside birds (the other biologist is primarily responsible for the smaller, inside birds). I don't have supervisory responsibility—all the keepers and biologists in the birdhouse report to an assistant curator—but part of my job is coordinating the day. Especially when the assistant curator is busy with other things. My particular expertise is Kori Bustards, a large, African bird. I've done a lot of research and have written papers about them. They're not particularly endangered and, in fact, there are about 200 of them in captivity. We have eight here at this zoo, including two babies. They're really amazing birds, and I've gotten to know each of them individually. They get to be as much as 40 pounds and typically live almost 30 years in captivity. The research I've done is all about how to improve their management in captivity, recommendations for pairing, and basically keeping track of them throughout the world.

WHY I MAJORED IN BIOLOGY

As a kid growing up, I loved animals and knew that I wanted to work with them. In fact, I even thought way back then that I wanted to work at a zoo. For a while I considered being a veterinarian, and so in high school I volunteered in a vet clinic. That actually taught me that I did not want to be a vet. I didn't want all that schooling. And I really didn't like seeing the animals in pain. I just couldn't deal with that. So I decided to major in biology—really just one area of it, zoology, because I knew all along that what I really wanted was to work in a zoo. I grew up in a small town, and we really didn't have a zoo. But I did visit larger ones, and that pretty much convinced me.

HOW THE BIOLOGY MAJOR PREPARED ME FOR MY JOB

I guess if I had to do it over, I would major in animal science, not biology, although certainly some of what I learned as a zoology major has helped me. In bio, I had to take a lot of the hard sciences like biochemistry, microbiology, chem., etc. I'm not sure that helped me that much in what I do now. Of course, I do research, so I needed to have an understanding of scientific method, statistics, scientific observation, and some of the other things you learn as a bio major. But as for caring for animals, well, you really don't learn much about that in college. I'm not suggesting that people who want to work in zoos skip college. It's just that if you really know you want to care for animals, there are other majors like animal science. Of course, I could have changed my mind and gone into veterinary science, and in that case, I really would have needed the bio background. But the courses I took in ornithology, animal behavior, evolution, and other mammal classes really helped.

OTHER TRAINING

I'd have to say that the most important training I've gotten is "on-the-job." There's really no other way to learn to be a zookeeper. You really have to do it. As I said, a good deal of my time is spent feeding the birds, cleaning the cage, even shoveling snow so the birds can get some fresh air and exercise. Obviously you don't go to college to learn that. But there's skill involved, and you learn from the other keepers. I left college for a little while and during that time, I volunteered at the zoo. That was the best training I ever got. They put me in the zoo hospital, and that was really, really hard. It was so depressing so I kept on looking for some other place. Then two biologist jobs opened up, one in the seal house and the other the birdhouse. I wanted the seal house because I really didn't know anything about birds. I didn't get that job and so took the birdhouse position. That's how a lot of keepers and biologists get their jobs. They volunteer. Then when a paid position opens up, you apply for it. We like to hire our volunteers because we know them and their work. They're already trained, and so it usually works out well. The interesting thing about being here is that I've really grown to love the birds, even though I didn't care for them when I got the job. I, of course, have grown very fond of the Kori's since I've spent so much time with them and learning about them. But I've also grown to love working at the birdhouse. It's interesting how that turned out. Now I continue to take courses about birds, specifically dealing with Kori's; I stay current on the literature and attend conferences to keep up.

HELPFUL MOVES

Obviously volunteering at the zoo was the best thing I ever did. But also volunteering at the vet clinic while I was in high school was a fantastic learning experience. Sure it taught me that I didn't want to be a vet. But it taught me so much more and exposed me to really working hands on with animals. Then, when I was volunteering at the zoo in the hospital, that really convinced me that I wanted to stay at the zoo, just not in the hospital. Another helpful thing I did was as a volunteer in high school. I was part of a hand rearing program where we actually helped raise some of the animals. So I guess what I'm saying is that for me, volunteering was a great way to break in and to learn what the life of a zookeeper is like.

PITFALLS TO AVOID

If I had to give someone advice about pitfalls to avoid, I'd say, don't eliminate any possibilities. A lot of people don't like reptiles or snakes, for example. But if a job opens up in that area, go for it. You'll learn a whole lot, and you'll have gotten your foot in the door. I'm not saying that someone who's really afraid of snakes or spiders should take a job like that. You'd probably be miserable. But don't eliminate a position in an area you don't know much about. It will very likely lead to other opportunities since there's always turnover.

WHAT I LOVE ABOUT MY JOB

No doubt about it, what I truly love about my job is working with the animals. In fact, just about every keeper has the same love. You certainly don't go into this field for the money. Keepers don't make very much. In fact, at some very small zoos, entry-level keepers make just a little over minimum wage. No, you go into this field because you absolutely love working with animals. You have day-to-day contact, and that's just so wonderful. Also, a new thing more and more zoos are getting into is training animals. Not like the training for circuses or pet training. But things like teaching the birds to land on a perch, which just happens to be a scale, so they can get weighed. We also have been teaching them to go inside a crate, so if they need to be transported, they don't get traumatized by being captured. I heard about a bird that had some form of respiratory problem and needed to breathe a mist every day. He was trained to stick his head in a tube that was connected to a mister. The training we do is about helping the animals.

THINGS ON THE JOB I COULD DO WITHOUT

For me, personally, I really hate to work in the rain. That's really no fun. But every zookeeper will tell you that the worst thing is when you lose an animal. You know it's going to happen. But when you work with them for years, it's a huge loss when they get sick or die. They're like pets to us. We know their personalities and so much about them. We have names for them, and so when one dies, we really feel the loss. In fact, when one of the high-profile animals died here, a famous animal, the staff was so upset that the administration brought in grief counselors to help us deal with it.

My Work and My Life

The thing about this job is that it can be very physical. Most people don't realize that. In fact, one of the requirements is that you have to be able to lift 100 pounds. You're carrying these big heavy hoses around; you're hauling straw, shoveling snow, cleaning—and in all kinds of weather: rain, snow, sleet, cold, hot. All of it. It's not just sitting around and watching the animals. There's always something different happening, and you're always on the go. Our hours are pretty regular. We work from early in the morning until about mid-afternoon. The whole staff leaves about 3:30 or so, except the vets who sometimes have to stay later. And we usually have to work weekends—*and* holidays—since that's when the zoo is visited most often. But it's all worth it, because you get to work day-to-day with the animals. This job is not for everyone. You either got it in you to work with animals or you don't.

Salaries for Zookeepers

Salaries for zookeepers, even those with degrees, are quite low as compared with other jobs in the field of biology. Entry-level zookeepers at very small zoos earn very little—some just a little more than minimum wage. Those with bachelor's and more advanced degrees earn about $40,000 to $50,000. As Sara said, you don't go into this field for money.

Some Thoughts About Sara's Career

Sara knew from her early years what she wanted to do in her life. She's unique that way. Most people don't know quite so early on. Nor quite so clearly. Sara also didn't get the job she wanted in the seal house and instead, wound up working with birds, about whom she had little knowledge. She grew to love her birds and her job, despite the sometimes hard physical work. Sara also worked hard to prove herself as a volunteer so that when a job opened, she had already had experience and the people who had the decision-making responsibility already knew she was a hard worker.

Rick, Science Reporter

In this case study, you meet Rick, a science reporter. As you read about Rick, please note some of the keys to his success that you might be in a position to emulate:

- ◆ He wasn't afraid to leave a lab job that he found unsatisfying to go to graduate school for a journalism degree and to explore his writing talents.

- ◆ He pursued an internship with a science magazine to establish writing samples.

- ◆ He left journalism to take a career in public relations and then left public relations to go back to journalism, which he found more interesting and challenging.

- ◆ He avoided being pigeon-holed in one area of science by keeping current with up-and-coming technologies, which gets him assigned to a wider scope of stories.

WHAT I DO

For the last several years, I've been a science reporter for one of the top newspapers in the country with a circulation of about a million and a readership several times that. My job is to write about science—mostly in the biology area since that's become my specialty—in a way that's accessible to people who may not know a lot about the subject but who are interested in it. At the same time, I also have to write for the people who truly understand the topic like the researchers, doctors, and professional journal folks. So not only must the story be understandable, it also has to be accurate. You can't compromise on accuracy just to make it easier to read.

WHY I MAJORED IN BIOLOGY

Believe it or not, it was all because of one great teacher! As a kid, I liked my chemistry set and enjoyed nature. But it was really because one teacher I had in high school made biology fun and interesting. I was particularly fascinated by parasites and insects. And then in college, I specialized in marine ecology—I was going to be the next Jacques Cousteau. But, of course, there was only one Cousteau. When I left college with my B.S. in bio, I worked for quite a while in a lab—not doing research. I was working in a hospital lab running tests on blood and tissue samples. Most of the work was for the ER doctors, and so the biggest challenge was to do all the tests quickly and, of course, accurately. Come to think of it, that's really not too different from what I do now. All my stories have to be accurate, and I have to write them quickly—usually in the afternoon or evening so they're in the morning paper.

HOW THE BIOLOGY MAJOR PREPARED ME FOR MY JOB

My bio background has both up- and downsides. On the upside is that I speak to a lot of scientists so having the background helps me understand more of what they're saying. That's not as true now as it was earlier in my career because the whole field of biology has changed so much since I learned it. When I was in school, there really was nothing about genetic splicing or nanotechnology. But at least my bio has helped me speak the same language as these scientists. On the downside, because of my background and interest, I sometimes get too involved in the details of the research, and I could miss some of the important questions that readers want answers to, like, "why is this important," or "did you know someone who had this disease, and that's why you became interested in this topic?" The human interest side of the story is what people want to read, and I have to be sure to write it.

OTHER TRAINING

I didn't start out as a reporter. In fact, when I first got out of college with my bio degree, I got a job working in a hospital lab. It was interesting for a while, but then it got very routine. Much of lab work is following recipes. There's not much creativity involved. It's still challenging, particularly when you have to run several different tests on a blood sample, for example, and you have to get the results back to the docs quickly. After a while, it just wasn't fulfilling for me so I started thinking about other things to do. Friends of mine suggested that I write about science since they thought I was a good writer. It's funny because they based that on all the letters and postcards I wrote to them when I'd be traveling. So I quit my job and went back to graduate school in journalism. That allowed me the chance to just write and do nothing else. I don't think it's necessary to go to journalism school. You can still be a good reporter learning the craft other ways. But it gave me a chance to do a lot of writing and get lots of feedback. That really helped me. After my two years of grad school, I did an internship, like many other journalism students. Mine was at a monthly science news magazine. It gave me a chance to do a lot of writing, but because it was a monthly, it was a bit slow. I eventually got hired by the magazine where I stayed a few years. After that I actually left the journalism side and went to work in public relations, sort of on the other side of the desk. Then, unlike most people who left journalism to work in PR, I actually went back into journalism, working for another monthly magazine. Then I got my current job at the newspaper. But even at this paper, I started writing for the weekly health section. It took a couple of years before a position opened in the daily news division, and I've been here eight or nine years now.

HELPFUL MOVES

To get a job in journalism you have to have "clips" (samples of your writing). I didn't have many until after I worked as an intern at the science magazine. That led to more work and more clips, which then established my credentials. Another helpful move was taking the PR job for a year and a half or so. Because it was at a major cancer hospital, I learned a great deal about cancer and how research gets done. I've been able to use that knowledge in talking with scientists. And it gave me an appreciation of what it's like on the other side. So when I get a press release or call about some research, I know to take it with a grain of salt.

PITFALLS TO AVOID

If there's one pitfall to avoid as a science reporter it's to be careful that you don't get typecast. You don't want to get too narrow in your focus or interest. Science reporting is already specialized. But you can get so narrow that you only get stories about AIDS, or psychology, or something. The key is to have a wider area of knowledge—and ability—so you get to do more stories about other interesting areas. For example, I decided that I wanted to learn more about nanotechnology because I felt this was an up and coming area. So I read as much as I could, and now I get to write the stories about that. I did the same with genetic engineering, so now I'm the gene guy. I didn't let myself get too specialized.

WHAT I LOVE ABOUT MY JOB

The first thing I can say about this has become a cliché in my field: I get paid to be in school and to always be learning something new. That means a lot to me. Also, with my credential at the newspaper, I can pretty much call up top scientists or academics and get them to talk to me about their work. Scientists don't usually get too much appreciation, so when I ask questions about them and their work, they just love to talk to me because I'm interested and enthusiastic. And what's even better is that I get to have a private tutorial from the person who best knows this particular topic. Another thing I can say here—and it's the reason I stopped doing lab work—is that there's so much creativity involved. That's an important part of this job. And I guess I have to say that I kind of enjoy being the first to hear about something and being the first to put it out. Even if it's just an hour before everyone else. There's kind of a cheap thrill getting so-called "inside information."

THINGS ON THE JOB I COULD DO WITHOUT

I could definitely do without the 11:00 P.M. calls from the editor! That's the time when the editors get to see the other major newspapers' stories. So they would call and ask why I didn't have this story. Or why we didn't have a particular part of it. It doesn't happen often, but it's not my favorite part of the job. Also, journalism is very, very competitive and stressful. There may be a breaking science story at five o'clock in the afternoon. I'll have to learn all about it, get all the background, talk to a lot of people, and write the story for the morning paper. Above all, the worst thing is the stress. Not so much having to put it all together in a short time. I can deal with that, and I even like some of it. It can be gratifying. The hardest part is making sure what you wrote is right! You're putting something out there for millions of people to read. That's scary. You really don't want to have to write a correction.

SALARIES FOR REPORTERS

The salaries for reporters are all over the map. Starting reporters on small newspapers (especially weekly papers) may make only about $20,000. Those with experience who work on large daily newspapers could earn salaries over $70,000. The median salary, however, would likely be in the $40,000 to $50,000 range for an experienced science reporter.

SOME THOUGHTS ABOUT RICK'S CAREER

It's heartening to hear that the reason Rick chose biology was one great teacher who turned him on to the subject. Most professionals can point to that one teacher who meant so much to them. What is particularly interesting about Rick's background and career choice is how he changed his direction quite a few years after he graduated from college. As a result, he went back to school to pursue the area he loved, writing. He was able to combine his two interests and, in fact, he even shares his two passions with his wife who is also a science reporter for a rival newspaper.

MY WORK AND MY LIFE

Life as a journalist is basically pushed to the end of the day. In the mornings you can read things and maybe follow up on the more in-depth stories you're working on. But as the day goes on, you start to get closer to the deadlines. Most of what I do is for the morning paper, and the stories don't usually take more than a day. There are lots of times when I'm working well into the evening. I'll be calling people on cell phones at dinner, in the evenings, whenever. They say that a journalist's rolodex is his lifeline. Well that's very true. That's where all your contacts and schmoozing come in. You have to be able to make contact with all your sources, sometimes at odd hours. You're always on deadline. Then in the morning, it starts all over.

Katie, Healthcare Attorney

In this case study, you meet Katie, an attorney who specializes in medical malpractice work. As you read about Katie, please note some of the keys to her success that you might be in a position to emulate:

◆ She did an internship at a pharmaceutical company, picking up knowledge about research.

◆ She took a risk by leaving a teaching job at a community college to go back to law school.

◆ She took time off after law school to search for a job while studying for her bar exam.

What I Do

I'm a litigator in a law firm that specializes in healthcare. Essentially, we defend healthcare providers in malpractice suits. My job requires going through a lot of medical records, talking to doctors and practitioners, and doing research on the conditions of the patients involved. In the state in which I live, which may be different from other states, cases involving malpractice have to go through a review process in front of a panel of three doctors who provide their expert opinions about the case. If they find merit, then the case will likely go to the next step, either to court, or settlement. You know, healthcare is not an exact science. There are no guarantees when it comes to treatment. This is obviously a time when trial attorneys are getting bad press. And, of course, some people might say I'm on the wrong side of the issue. I should be defending the plaintiff, not the healthcare providers. But my feeling is that everyone has a right to a good defense. We do that in the criminal justice system, and this is no different.

Why I Majored in Biology

My whole childhood, I was the "science fair queen." I loved science and entered all the fairs since about fourth grade. My father was a research scientist at a pharmaceutical company, so I grew up in that atmosphere. In fact, I even did an internship at his company one summer. When I was going to school, if you loved science, especially biology, you usually became a doctor. In fact, my sister became a doctor and for a while I thought about it, too. But I guess I really wasn't cut out for that kind of work. My sister is a natural for it, but not me. When I discovered research, I just knew that's what I wanted to do, although in high school I also loved my government class, and my teacher encouraged me to go to law school. Ultimately, she was right since that's where I've ended up. But I took a few other turns before getting here.

When I got to college, I loved both biology and chemistry, so I actually wound up majoring in both, that is, biochemistry. And I went on to graduate school in biochem, too.

How the Biology Major Prepared Me for My Job

My background in biology and chemistry helps a lot. For my cases, I do a lot of research, reviewing medical records, and talking to doctors about cases and issues. I actually worked in science for quite a while before going to law school and that helps me understand the issues a lot better than some other attorneys. It gives me an edge. But what's interesting is that now more and more attorneys have science backgrounds, particularly in the kind of law I do. In fact, there are some attorneys who are also medical doctors. And I know that there are some combination medicine and law programs. When I was in law school, I thought I wanted to go into patent law, which also would have been a good thing with my science background. But being in patent law meant that I would have had to move to one of the major cities, and I wanted to stay closer to home. I was able to find a local law firm that specialized in health insurance defense work. I've since moved to another firm, but I'm still involved in healthcare law.

OTHER TRAINING

During summers while I was in college I did a couple of internships, one in fact at my father's company. In one internship I did research on miscarriages, trying to learn more about why they happen. We were specifically looking at embryonic rejection. In fact, I continued that research as a graduate student and wrote my thesis on it. After college I went to grad school in biochemistry, which was housed in the Physiology department. I got my Master of Science in Physiology and Biophysics and left before I finished my Ph.D. Right after that, I started teaching science at the local community college. Mostly I taught anatomy and physiology to nursing students. I enjoyed it a great deal, but it didn't feel like the right career for me. My roommate was a law student and we talked about me going into law, too. So I signed up to take the Law School Admission Test (LSAT) almost on a lark, although I did study hard for it. I did quite well so I was accepted into a couple of good law schools. I was still teaching at the community college at the time, and one of my options was to go to school part time and continue working. I decided that wasn't the best thing for me, so I quit my job and went to school full time. That was a smart decision.

HELPFUL MOVES

After I finished law school, I didn't have a job. As I said, I had thought about becoming a patent law attorney, but I'd have had to move and take a second exam in patent law so I decided that wasn't for me. Also first I had to pass the bar. So during the summer after I graduated, I came home, studied for the bar, and started interviewing for jobs nearby. I came across an ad in the paper for an attorney at a small law firm specializing in health insurance defense work. With my back-ground, I was able to get the job, and I stayed there for a number of years before moving to my current firm. It's larger, and I have a little more diverse kind of practice here.

PITFALLS TO AVOID

I would tell people who are interested in being a lawyer that they shouldn't focus too much—or too early. There are lots of areas of the law, or in the sciences, too, for that matter. You don't want to get pigeon-holed. You don't have to go into healthcare law. You don't necessarily know what you want right away, so when you're in school, that's a good time to try out different areas.

WHAT I LOVE ABOUT MY JOB

What's wonderful about my current job is that it's always different. Even though the firm specializes in healthcare, and I have a specific expertise, I never really know what will come across my desk. It could be an obstetrical cases or something involving orthopedics. Or it could be a simple slip-and-fall case. That makes the job very exciting. And I get to meet a lot of new people all the time who are interesting.

THINGS ON THE JOB I COULD DO WITHOUT

I could do without the stress of maintaining my billable hours. But that's really part of the job, so I can't. But there's a lot of stress involved. Another part of the job I could do without is "development." That's the part where you're out looking for cases. There's usually a lot of wining and dining you have to do to make sure you're on top of things and aware of situations. I'm not really the sales-type, but a lot of being an attorney is making sure there are new cases.

MY WORK AND MY LIFE

Although I love my job, my family and community were always more important to me than my career. That's one of the main reasons why I didn't go into patent law. I wanted to stay near my home and not go to New York or some other major city. Also, a nice thing about my work is that the hours aren't too crazy, unlike many attorneys in the big law firms. Sometimes they have to work very late hours, seven days a week. My hours aren't anywhere near that bad. I work from about 8 in the morning until about 6. Yes, I usually have to work on the weekends, too, but not all day. I get to do some traveling, too, but the kind of travel I do is short trips. I may be on the road about 15 percent of the time. But mostly they're day trips where I'll drive to another city and be back the same night.

SALARIES FOR ATTORNEYS

Attorneys are some of the highest paid professionals in the world. Some attorneys just out of law school earn $125,000 or more a year. Those are the graduates from the most prestigious law schools who work at the large law firms in the major cities. More typically, starting lawyers earn $60,000 to $80,000.

SOME THOUGHTS ABOUT KATIE'S CAREER

Katie decided that her lifestyle was more important than her success. She could have gone to one of the major law firms in a large city and earned a great deal of money as a patent attorney. Instead, she decided that she wanted to stay near her home and practice law there. Her background in biology helped her secure a law job in insurance and over time she was able to transition to her current job. She hasn't had to compromise her life goals and even when she travels she manages to get home the same day. While trial lawyers have certainly been under great political pressure recently, and healthcare providers are often considered "the enemy," Katie's attitude is firm that everyone deserves a good defense. Healthcare providers are not always wrong, and it's her job to make sure the truth wins out.

Gail, Technical Director, Hospital Laboratory

In this case study, you are introduced to Gail, the technical director of a hospital laboratory. As you read about Gail, please note some of the keys to her success that you might be in a position to emulate:

- ◆ She was focused on job possibilities and her future prospects before choosing her major and specialty.

- ◆ She took a night-shift lab job to get her feet in the door.

- ◆ She continues her education and training by taking management courses, which help supplement her medical technician training.

WHAT I DO

My official title is Technical Director of the hospital laboratory. What that means is that I'm in charge of the entire hospital lab, which consists of about 30 medical technologists and technicians, 10 phlebotomists, and 15 support staff. That's about 55 people, so a lot of my job involves managing people, troubleshooting, and quality control. QC is probably one of the most important parts of the job because everything in the hospital is dependent on our tests being accurate. But working with people probably takes up most of my time.

WHY I MAJORED IN BIOLOGY

I grew up in the Philippines where almost everyone went to college. There are eight children in my family; my father was a general in the army; and my mother stayed at home to bring up the kids. We were all expected to do well in school and to go on to college. One of my brothers became a doctor, another a dentist, and one of my sisters became a nurse. It's very competitive in the Philippines, so when you go to college, you have to be very aware of whether there will be a job for you when you finish. I didn't really know what I wanted to take—I knew I didn't want anything dealing with business, commerce, or marketing. And I always did well in science, so I thought I'd start there. I was pretty shy as a kid and preferred to be in the background. That's changed now that I'm a manager, but it's how I started out. I never thought about being a doctor because of that. Like most of the students I took all the basic courses in science, and I found that I really liked anatomy and physiology and chemistry. I wasn't sure whether to choose bio or chem, and then I discovered that I could do both by taking medical technology, which was part of the bio department. In the Philippines, so many people have degrees that it's hard to find a good job after you graduate. There, there are more workers than jobs. I knew that being a med tech would lead to a job. My future was always on my mind.

HOW THE BIOLOGY MAJOR PREPARED ME FOR MY JOB

Well, of course, being in charge of the lab means I have to know what everyone does. And in order to be a good manager, I need to know how the system works. With my background in biology and chemistry, and the years I spent "working the bench," I know how the people in the lab are thinking. When I first came here from the Philippines, I started working in a doctor's office lab. When I moved to a large hospital, I worked in hematology, and at this hospital I started in chemistry. I've worked in a lot of specific areas of med tech so I know a lot about what the med techs do here at this hospital.

OTHER TRAINING

When I came to the United States. I had to have my transcript evaluated before I could get a job as a med tech. And I had to work for several years before I could be registered. I also had to pass a test. As for management, well, a lot of my current job is "on-the-job-training." I've taken seminars and management classes periodically. In fact, I'll be taking another course next year and would love to be able to get my master's degree in health management. But there's too much going on in the lab to do that right now. I think it's important to keep taking these courses to get an edge. In hospital administration, you have to prove yourself to be indispensable.

HELPFUL MOVES

I'd have to say that I was pretty lucky. I was basically in the right place at the right time. When I first came to this hospital, I started working the night shift. That was tough, but it's what I had to do to get a good job. After a while, I heard they were looking for a day-shift supervisor in chemistry, so I applied. I got the job, but, at the same time, there was an opening for an assistant technical director. I applied for that as well and, as it turns out, wound up doing both assistant technical director and day-shift supervisor at the same time. A few years later, the tech director left, so I applied and got the job. Just being here helped me know about the job openings. I think I was able to get these jobs because I really understand what the people in the lab do and how hard and challenging these jobs are.

PITFALLS TO AVOID

To be a good manager, you have to have a lot of patience. You need the right attitude to make your impact. I can't think of it as "my" lab. That's too selfish and self-centered. I also think the key to success in management is sincerity. Too many managers don't let that come through. To be a good manager, you have treat each person differently because they're all individuals. That can be very time consuming, but it's worth the time. You also have to be consistent with people and think of the entire lab. My job is not to do things to be liked, that is, for popularity, but to be respected. Everything we do, every decision we make has to be for the good of the lab as a whole. The staff has to see that. Another thing about management, especially in a hospital setting, is that you have to think progressively. This is not a place for old management styles.

WHAT I LOVE ABOUT MY JOB

You really make a difference here. When you work in healthcare, especially in a hospital, you affect the lives of people so much because inherently, you're helping someone. As a med tech, it's not directly, of course. But all the work we do is for patients, even though we rarely, if ever, see them. Another thing about being a med tech, or even a health administrator is that you don't go into it for money. You do it because you care. Managing people is hard and challenging, but the outcome of all that work is a great feeling when things at the lab are going well. We have a happy group here, and that provides fulfillment for me.

THINGS ON THE JOB I COULD DO WITHOUT

Paperwork, of course. But you have to do it. Especially in this job. We have to keep track of everything. Also, this is a for-profit hospital so I'm held accountable for all the money we spend. I know there's waste in some areas of the hospital. That's frustrating, because I don't think we're guilty of waste, yet we don't have enough staff to do our jobs as well as I'd like. I'm held accountable for everything, and when anything goes wrong, it's my fault. That's just part of the job, I guess.

MY WORK AND MY LIFE

To do this job well, you have to be really well organized, otherwise you'd live here. You'd never be able to leave at night. This is a very high-pressure job; you feel it from all sides. Everything here has to be done immediately, and it always has to be accurate. So quality control is so important. I'm also a cheerleader for the lab, which can sometimes be hard. For the most part, though, unless there's some big project going on or we're about to undergo a big inspection, my hours are pretty regular and reasonable. I work about 8 hours, but it's really because I'm very organized and good at time management. The hospital has doubled in size since I've been here, and we've recently expanded our service. I have a good staff; we're a happy group; and I don't have a problem taking on the accountability that comes with being a manager.

SALARIES FOR EPIDEMIOLOGISTS

Salaries for starting medical technologists range from about $40,000 to $50,000. As one gains experience and moves up the career ladder, salaries can be significantly higher, especially in large metropolitan areas and large hospitals. Senior laboratory personnel with supervisory responsibility are often considered management and, therefore, can earn well over $100,000.

SOME THOUGHTS ABOUT GAIL'S CAREER

Gail came from a family where everyone went into some area of science. She chose medical technology but could have just as easily chosen to be a doctor. But Gail had to start over when she immigrated to the United States. She was quite focused on doing excellent work and was willing to take the night shift just so she could get the job. She says that she was just "in the right place at the right time." But in truth, her promotion to director is not a result of serendipity but of her hard work for an extended period of time. There usually is no short cut and just by being in the right place does not guarantee anything. The hospital and the lab are both growing quickly and Gail is given a great deal of credit by management for the smooth way the lab has handled the growth. She, in turn, says that it's because of the staff. Her attitude toward her staff have contributed to the success of the lab and she realizes that she needs to keep learning to become an even better manager.

Chapter 7

Final Thoughts

Throughout this book there has been one consistent theme, and that is choice. You have choices in all the decisions you make about your education and afterward: your college, your major, and your career choices.

First, when you are in the process of evaluating colleges, you should look at all your options. Many colleges can offer you a quality education. Your task is to choose from among those that meet your selection criteria. Naturally you will want to make sure the college offers the classes and programs you want, both within the biology department and in the other academic areas that interest you. But you will also want to make sure that the college is a good fit for you. Rankings tell you little about fit. Factors such as size, location, and type of school should weigh equally with the degree of selectivity or academic reputation. Ultimately, it will be your choice. I hope this book also demonstrates that ability to pay should not be one of the factors in that decision. Financial aid should make even the most expensive college affordable.

Second, when you are selecting your major, you should keep your options open. Ask yourself whether you are committed to biology or whether there are other disciplines in which you have a strong interest. Remember that you can major in more than one academic area as a double major, or you can major in one and minor in another. It's important that you learn about the different disciplines of biology before deciding on your area of specialty. I hope this book helps you realize that you have many options.

Third, as the time approaches for you to graduate from college, several options are open to you. One of those options is pursuing an advanced degree in biology. When you choose that path, you will have to know the area in which you will specialize since most graduate programs expect you to focus on one discipline. By the time you are considering graduate school, it is very likely you will have already chosen that direction. Often that will dictate to which graduate school you will apply. But options remain even at that point, and you have choices to make. Also, don't forget to use the same selection criteria you used when choosing your undergraduate school. Fit, location, and size are just as important for graduate schools, perhaps even more so.

For those who are ready to pursue their careers, I hope I have opened up a whole array of options for you in which you can use your knowledge and experience in biology. The six case studies all majored in biology, yet each pursued a different path. Karen, the epidemiologist, and Sara, the zookeeper, continue to use biology on a daily basis. Some do not, like Gail, the technical director of a hospital lab, and Katie, the healthcare attorney. And some, like Rick, the science reporter, and Susan, the outreach coordinator, changed directions.

The point is, you have choices: in which school you attend, in which subject you choose as your major, and in your career options. Above all, none of these choices are final—unless you want them to be. And that, too, is your choice.

Resources

Biology Honor Society

Beta Beta Beta (Tri-beta) is a national biological honor society with chapters on many college campuses. Its purpose is to recognize and promote outstanding achievement in the biological sciences. BBB participates in both academic and social activities throughout the school year. One of its primary goals is to offer the opportunity for members to interact with the biology community on campus. The meetings provide students with the chance to speak with professors and fellow students outside the classroom and to discuss the pros and cons of various classes. Some chapters also have guest speakers at meetings, which can help you remain informed about academic and extracurricular possibilities open to you. Membership on many campuses is restricted based on academic grades and recommendations from faculty.

Professional Resources

Within the field of biology are professional societies for just about every kind of specialty. These organizations are made up of professionals in the field and serve various purposes, among them collegiality, information dissemination, and serving as a clearinghouse for job openings. Many of these organizations have student memberships, and they provide great opportunities for students to get jobs and become part of the professional biology community.

THE AMERICAN INSTITUTE OF BIOLOGICAL SCIENCES (AIBS)

The American Institute of Biological Sciences is an umbrella organization for the biological sciences. It is an independent nonprofit organization that represents more than 80 professional societies and organizations with a combined membership exceeding 240,000 scientists and educators. See www.aibs.org for more information.

PROFESSIONAL SOCIETIES

Following are a number of professional societies whose members are specific to the field. To contact them, you can go directly to the Web site shown or use a search engine to find them.

American Association for Plant Taxonomists (www.sysbot.org)

American Fisheries Society (www.fisheries.org)

American Genetic Association (www.theaga.org)

American Society for Cell Biology (www.ascb.org)

American Society for Horticultural Science (www.ashs.org)

The American Society for Microbiology (www.asmusa.org)

American Society of Agronomy (www.crops.org)

American Society of Human Genetics (http://genetics.faseb.org)

Animal Behavior Society (www.animalbehavior.org)

The Association of Biomolecular Resource Facilities (www.abrf.org)

Botanical Society of America (www.botany.org)

Federation of American Societies for Experimental Biology (www.faseb.org)

Society for Conservation Biology (www.conbio.org)

Society for Economic Botany (www.econbot.org)

Society for Industrial Microbiology (www.simhq.org)

Society for Integrative and Comparative Biology (www.sicb.org)

Job Listing Web Sites

You can find a wealth of job-related sites on the Internet. Some provide job listings that you can search; some provide job postings, where you can post your resume for employers looking to fill positions. Most sites provide career advice. And most provide a combination of these various services. In some, you can search for jobs under biology.

Often the best place to find jobs in biology is the newspaper want ads (online), particularly in major metropolitan areas. In addition to the local and large city newspapers, you should also check the *Washington Post* want ads (www.washingtonpost.com) because many associations in the area advertise in the *Post*. The government also advertises in the *Post*, but you should be sure to check the official government job listing Web site www.usajobs.opm.gov.

The most well-known job site is www.monster.com. This site enables you to search for jobs, network with its other members, get career advice, and post your résumé. To search for jobs, you must sign up for a free monster account. You then can choose to receive email updates.

Another job site is www.craigslist.com. This site has grown tremendously in recent years. You can check jobs available in each city or do a search. You can also post your résumé for potential employers.

Often the most helpful Web sites are the local newspaper job listings. You can do searches by key words, and in many locales, you can post your résumé, just as with monster and craigslist.

www.careerbuilder.com claims "900,000 jobs, The Internet's Largest Job Search & Employment site." You can search for jobs, post résumés, get advice, find resources, and get information about career fairs.

www.collegegrad.com focuses on finding entry-level jobs and includes help for preparing résumés, cover letters, interviews, and more.

Try looking for sites that focus on a particular type of job. For instance, you can find online job clubs or career sites dedicated to a particular field. For example, www.biologyjobs.com and www.sciencejobs.com.

And, of course, there is always the ultimate search engine: Google.

College Admission, Search, and Financial Aid Resources

Many resources are available to help you choose and apply to college. Many of these will also provide excellent information about financing your education and will help you apply for financial aid. Some of these also provide *free* scholarship search. (*Note:* you should *never* pay for a search of available scholarships. Nor should you pay to have your financial aid applications completed by an organization.)

Following is a partial list of the organizations and their Web sites that are related to college admission and financial aid. Once again, you can do your own search at Google or use the search engine of your choice!

U.S. Department of Education (www.ed.gov)

The College Board (www.collegeboard.com)

FAFSA on the Web (www.fafsa.ed.gov)

FinAid! The SmartStudent Guide to Financial Aid (www.finaid.org)

FastWeb (www.fastweb.com)

American Educational Guidance Center (www.college-scholarships.com)

College Net (www.collegenet.com)

College View (www.collegeview.com)

Financial Aid Resource Center (www.theoldschool.org)

Peterson's Financial Aid Center (www.petersons.com)

Student Loan Marketing Assn. (Sallie Mae) (www.salliemae.com)

National Association of Student Financial Aid Administrators (www.nasfaa.org)

Educational Testing Service (www.ets.org)

American College Testing (www.act.org)

Students.Gov (www.students.gov)

How Stuff Works (www.howstuffworks.com)

CollegeView (www.collegeview.com)

GradView (www.gradview.com)

Biology Career Reference Books

If you don't have online access or you prefer to do your research at a library or bookstore, you still have a lot of help available. Following are some printed references, which you might find helpful.

Brown, Sheldon. *Opportunities in Biotechnology Careers,* McGraw-Hill, 2000.

Camenson, Blythe. *Great Jobs for Biology Majors,* McGraw-Hill, 2003.

The College Board. *The College Board Index of Majors & Graduate Degrees 2004,* The College Board, 2003.

The College Board. *The College Handbook*, The College Board, 2004.

Fiske, Peter S. and Louie, Aaron. *Put Your Science to Work: The Take-Charge Career Guide for Scientists,* American Geophysical Union, 2001.

Kreeger, Karen Young. *Guide to Nontraditional Careers in Science,* Taylor & Francis Group, 1998.

Landis Andrews, Linda. *How to Choose a College Major,* McGraw-Hill, 1997.

Louise, Chandra B. *Jump Start Your Career in BioScience,* Peer Productions, 1998.

Machado, Julio. *Fishing for a Major (Students Helping Students),* Natavi Guides, 2003.

Maynard, Thane and Goodall, Jane. *Working with Wildlife: A Guide to Careers in the Animal World,* Franklin Watts, 2000.

Miller, Louise. *Careers for Animal Lovers & Other Zoological Types,* McGraw-Hill, 2000.

Thomson Peterson's. *Peterson's Four-Year Colleges*, Thomson Peterson's, 2004.

Princeton Review. *The Guide to College Majors: Deciding the Right Major and Choosing the Best School,* Princeton, 2002.

Quintana, Debra. *100 Jobs in the Environment,* Macmillan, 1997.

Robbins-Roth, Cynthia. *Alternative Careers in Science,* Academic Press, 1998.

Rugg, Frederick E. *Rugg's Recommendations on the Colleges,* 2004.

Viollt, Michael. *College Majors That Work: A Step-by-Step Guide to Choosing and Using Your College Major,* Octameron Associates, 2004.

Wetfeet. *Careers in Biotech & Pharmaceuticals: The WetFeet Insider Guide,* Wetfeet, 2004.

Winter, Charles. *Opportunities in Biological Science Careers,* McGraw-Hill, 2004.

Index

A

ACT tests
    scores, 24–25
    taking multiple times, 25
admissions
    elements, 23–27
    essay and, 25
    extracurricular activities and,
      25–26
    grad school, 45–46
    reasons, 27
    recommendations and, 26–27
    resources, 122–123
    test scores and, 24–25
    transcript and, 23–24
advisors, meeting with, 51
agronomist, 57
American Institute of Biological
  Sciences (AIBS), 120
animal scientists, 62
applications
    deadlines, 22
    essay/personal statement, 25
    extracurricular activities, 25–26
    important elements, 23–27
    recommendations, 26–27
    test scores, 24–25
    transcript, 23–24
aquatic biologists, 59
archivists, 58
attorneys, 107–111
audiologists, 64–65

B

Bachelor of Arts (B.A.). *See also*
  degrees; majors
    precollege courses, 17
    requirements, 9
    salaries, 48
Bachelor of Science (B.S.). *See also*
  degrees; majors
    precollege courses, 17
    requirements, 9–10
    salaries, 48
Beta Beta Beta (BBB), 119
biochemistry
    graduate schools, 44
    highly selective colleges, 15
    less selective colleges, 15
biochemists, 59
biological sciences
    degrees and curricula, 8–11
    fields of study, 8
    graduate schools, 44
    minor in, 11–12
    subspecialties, 8
biologists. *See also* careers
    aquatic, 59
    biochemist, 59
    biophysicist, 60
    botanist, 59–60
    ecologist, 60
    microbiologist, 60
    physiologist, 60
    salaries, 59
    zoologist, 60

biology
    career reference books, 123–124
    graduate school programs, 39–40
    highly selective colleges, 14
    internships, 36–39
    less selective colleges, 14–15
biology majors
    B.A., 9, 17, 48
    B.S., 9–10, 17, 48
    college selection for, 21–34
    double majors and, 12
    skills/abilities requirement, 17–18
biomedical engineers, 65
biophysicists, 60
books and supplies, 30
botanists, 59–60

C

career fairs, 80–81
CareerBuilder.com, 121
careers
    agronomist, 57
    animal scientist, 62
    archivist, curator, museum
        technician, 58
    audiologist, 64–65
    biologist, 59–60
    biomedical engineer, 65
    chiropractor, 64
    dietitian, 58
    education and outreach program
        manager, 93–97
    environmental scientist, 61
    epidemiologist, 87–92
    food scientist, 56, 61–62
    forensic scientist, 56–57
    forester, 54
    health scientist administrator, 54
    healthcare attorney, 107–111
    hospital laboratory director,
        111–115
    medical instrument technician, 54
    medical librarian, 62–63
    medical technologist, 54–55
    medical writer, 57

    nutritionist, 58
    options, 118
    optometrist, 63
    park guide, 56
    patent examiner, 55
    pharmacist, 65–66
    pharmacologist/toxologist, 56
    podiatrist, 63–64
    public relations, pharmaceuticals,
        57
    quarantine officer, 55
    sales representative, 58–59
    sanitarian, 55
    science reporter, 102–107
    zookeeper, 97–102
case studies
    education and outreach program
        manager, 93–97
    epidemiologist, 87–92
    healthcare attorney, 107–111
    hospital laboratory director,
        111–115
    science reporter, 102–103
    zookeeper/biologist, 97–102
cell biology, graduate schools, 44
chiropractors, 64
CollegeGrad.com, 121
colleges
    benefits, 32
    biochemistry majors, 15
    biology majors, 14–15
    biology program offerings, 13–16
    choosing, 21–34
    entrance requirements, 16–17
    evaluation, 117
    graduation options, 118
    paying for, 27–30
    prestige, 22
    rankings, 13
    Web sites, locating, 11
    zoology majors, 16
community college instructors, 40
companies
    interview focus, 84
    overview Web sites, 83
    researching, 82–83

contacts
        finding, 75–76
        maintaining, 76–77
contingency employment, 75
cost of attendance. *See also* financial aid
        books and supplies, 30
        college worth, 31–32
        elements, 29
        need and, 28
        net cost versus, 31
        room and board, 30
CraigsList.com, 121
curators, 58

D

deadlines, 46
degrees
        B.A., 9
        B.S., 9–10
        master's, 41
        Ph.D., 41
        requirements, 9, 10
        types of, 8
demographic trends, 82
dietitians, 58
doctors of chiropractic, 64
doctors of optometry, 63
doctors of podiatric medicine
    (DPMs), 63
double majors, 12

E

ecologists, 60
economic trends, 82
education and outreach program
    manager, case study, 93–97
Education Pays, 32
employees, top 10 characteristics, 68
employment
        agencies, 72
        contingency, 75
entrance requirements, 16–17
entry-level positions, 81
environmental scientists, 61

epidemiologist, case study, 87–92
essays, 25
extracurricular activities, 25–26

F

financial aid
        access and, 27–28
        cost of attendance and, 29–30
        foundation, 27
        grad school, 46–47
        need determination and, 29
        resources, 122–123
        types, 30–31
food scientists, 56, 61–62
forensic scientists, 56–57
foresters, 54

G

Graduate Record Exam (GRE), 45, 50
graduate schools
        admission, 45–46
        biochemistry, 44
        biological sciences, 44
        biology programs, 39–40
        cell biology, 44
        community college instructors, 40
        competition, 46
        deadlines, 46
        disciplines, 40–41
        financial aid, 46–47
        financial benefits, 48–49
        highly ranked, 44–45
        interdisciplinary approach, 41
        master's degree programs, 41
        microbiology, 44
        molecular biology, 45
        paying for, 46–49
        Ph.D. programs, 41
        quality programs, 42–45
        selection criteria, 42
        selective, 43
        student loans, 48
graduates, quality of life, 32
GRE (Graduate Record Exam), 45, 50

H

Harvard University, 43
health scientist administrators, 54
healthcare attorney, case study, 107–111
home-schooled students, 23–24
hospital laboratory director, case study
    111–115

I

Internet job search. *See* online job search
internships
    availability, 36
    benefits, 36, 37
    in career decision-making, 37
    companies, contacting, 38–39
    competition, 39
    as fellowships, 38
    finding, 38–39
    links, 39
    payment, 38
interviews
    experience, using, 86
    follow-up, 85–86
    notes, 85
    practicing, 83–84
    process, 85
    questions, 84–85
    research, 82–83
    tips, 84
    typical questions, 83

J

job descriptions. *See* careers
job listing Web sites, 39, 121
job search
    basics, 69
    book, 70–71
    changing workplace and, 74–75
    clichés, 71–72
    company downsizing and, 73–74
    contingency employment and, 75
    employment agencies, 72
    first contact results, 71

information organization, 71
    informed, 72–73
    networks, 75–77
    with on-campus recruiters, 80–81
    online, 72, 77–78
    planning for, 68–69
    realistic, 72–73
    resources, 122–123
    résumé preparation, 78–80
    schedule, 71–72
    skills/knowledge, 67
    tasks, time calculation, 70
    time, budgeting, 69–70
    trends and, 73–75
    underemployment, 74
jobs
    interviewing for, 82–86
    openings, finding, 81–82
    trends, 82

M

majors
    B.A., 9, 17, 48
    B.S., 9–10, 17, 48
    college selection and, 21–34
    double, 12
    selecting, 117
    skills/abilities requirement, 17–18
master's degree
    programs, 41
    salaries, 48–49
medical instrument technicians, 54
medical librarians, 62–63
medical technologists, 54–55
medical writers, 57
microbiologists, 60
microbiology, graduate schools, 44
minors
    in biological sciences, 11–12
    in other departments, 12
MIT, 42, 43
molecular biology, graduate schools, 45
Monster.com, 121
museum technicians, 58

N

need
    cost of attendance and, 28
    determining, 29
net cost, 31
networks
    how to use, 75–77
    maintaining, 76–77
    social, 76
    volunteering and, 76
nutritionists, 58

O

on-campus recruiters, 80–81
online job search. *See also* job search
    advantages/disadvantages, 77
    data, sending, 78
    information, 78
    in search schedule, 72
optometrists, 63

P

parents
    conversation, 21
    as mirror, 22
    support, 22
park guides, 56
patent examiners, 55
Ph.D.
    programs, 41
    salaries, 49
pharmacists, 65–66
pharmacologists/toxologists, 56
physiologists, 60
podiatrists, 63–64
precollege courses, 17
private scholarships, 33
professional resources, 119–120
public relations, pharmaceuticals, 57

Q

quarantine officers, 55

R

recommendations
    defined, 26
    writers of, 26–27
recruiters, 80–81
research, job interview, 82–83
resources
    biology career reference, 123–124
    biology honor society, 119
    college admission, 122–123
    financial aid, 122–123
    job listing Web sites, 121
    professional, 119–120
    search, 122–123
    societies, 120
résumés
    activities, 79
    preparing, 78–80
    resources, 79
    suggestions, 78–79
    work experiences, 79
room and board, 30

S

salaries
    agronomist, 57
    animal scientist, 62
    archivist, 58
    audiologist, 65
    bachelor's degree, 48
    biologist, 59
    biomedical engineer, 65
    chiropractor, 64
    curator, 58
    dietitian and nutritionist, 58
    education and outreach program
        manager, 96
    epidemiologist, 92
    food scientist, 56, 62
    forensic scientist, 56–57
    forester, 54
    health scientist administrator, 54
    healthcare attorney, 107–111
    hospital laboratory director, 115

salaries *(continued)*
  master's degree, 48–49
  medical instrument technician, 54
  medical librarian, 63
  medical technologist, 54–55, 115
  medical writer, 57
  museum technician, 58
  optometrist, 63
  park guide, 56
  patent examiner, 55
  Ph.D., 49
  pharmacist, 66
  pharmacologist/toxologist, 56
  podiatrist, 64
  public relations, pharmaceuticals,
    57
  quarantine officer, 55
  sales representative, 58–59
  sanitarian, 55
  science reporter, 106
  zookeeper, 101
sales representatives, 58–59
sanitarians, 55
SAT tests
  scores, 24–25
  taking multiple times, 25
scholarships
  private, 33
  search firms, 33–34
  warning, 33–34
science reporter, case study, 102–107
skills/abilities, 17–18
social networks, 76
Stanford University, 42, 43
student loans. *See also* financial aid
  consolidation, 47
  grad students, 48
students
  home-schooled, 23–24
  honesty, 22
  organization, 22
  power, 23

T

technical director, hospital laboratory,
  case study, 111–115
test scores
  admissions and, 24–25
  high, 24
  low, 24
toxologists, 56
transcripts. *See also* admissions
  as dynamic, multidimensional
    documents, 23
  home-schooled students and,
    23–24
tuition/fees, in estimated budgets, 30

U

underemployment, 74
University of Wisconsin, 43

V

volunteer work, 76

W

Web sites
  college, 11
  company overview, 83
  job listing, 39, 121
  professional societies, 120
wildlife biologists, 60

Z

zookeeper, case study, 97–102
zoologists, 60
zoology, 16